Grantastic!

Gran

For Michael

When the grandmothers speak the earth will be healed.

Old Hopi Indian saying

Contents

Acknowledgments

Thank you, Shirley Conran, for thinking of the joyously upbeat title, Grantastic! Only what I'd expect from Superwoman.

Thank you to all the grandmothers, friends and relatives who shared their anecdotes, experiences and views. These include Joan Bakewell, Craig Brown, Cynthia and George Brown, Molly Dineen, Dirk Fieldhouse, Angela Flowers, Mary and Dick Francis, Barbara Follett MP, Ruth Gorb, Anna Haycraft, Jenny Henderson, Angela Ince, Madhur Jaffrey, Kathy Jager, Rochelle Kennaway, Leslie Kenton, Joy McWatters, Monica Offer, Prunella Scales, Audrey Slaughter, Penny Vincenzi and Katharine Whitehorn.

Thank you to the journalists and authors who wrote the perfect paragraph while I was still searching for the right words and who are therefore included in these chapters – Eugenie Bryan, Jeanne Davis, Terry Durack, Jo Joseph, Sheila Kitzinger, India Knight, Leanda de Lisle, Julie Myerson, Catherine O'Brien, Mark Steyn,

Professor Laurie Taylor and Dr Ruth Westheimer.

Thank you, Judith Longman and Rebecca Russel Ponte of Hodder & Stoughton, and my agent, Carole Blake, for being so helpful and efficient.

And thank you, Merrily Harpur, for the witty, skilful drawings and cartoons.

Shirley Lowe

Preface

My friend Marcia phoned the other day to tell me that her daughter was pregnant. 'I can't possibly be a grandmother,' she said. 'I go to the gym three days a week *and* I dye my hair.'

I reminded her that grandmothers no longer come shawl-wrapped, accessorised with rocking chairs and knitting needles. These days they are more likely to be designer-clad (watch out for small, sticky fingers on the DKNY) and, what with all the exercises and yoga, helpful line-reducing creams and subtle make-up, grandmothers these days are pleased to be mistaken for their daughters when they have time to wheel out the pram.

You'd think that this aerobically taut generation with their competitive careers and crisp confidence would have the whole grandmother thing efficiently under control, but you'd be wrong. Today's grannies may choose to block out the noise of children at play by switching on their Walkman instead of turning off their hearing aids but they are, nevertheless, out of date and out of touch, poor old things. ('It's not the same as it was in your day, you know, mummy.')

Old-fashioned is how grandparents are destined to be, as each new batch of parents formats its own rules ('Cosmo isn't allowed to play with guns, mummy'), swears by its own products ('You did remember to put the Soother in the steam steriliser, didn't you, mum?') and follows its own childcare gurus. The current lot of experts, incidentally, have hot views on allergies and asthma and don't talk about Quality Time much any more. This, as you will soon discover, is because *all* time is Quality Time; the children are always with you.

Most modern parents seem terribly keen on this and naturally assume that you, the proud grandparents, will be equally delighted to entertain babies and toddlers for a full day shift and be as charmed as they are by the amusing way your ten-months-old grandchild, from the vantage point of his highchair, is able to spit a mouthful of cereal right across the dinner table at grandpa.

Their perception of a grandmother goes right back to that stereotypical image of the loveable old dear in the shawl, nodding indulgently at a four-year-old having a temper tantrum. 'I'll bring Jonathan over to you nice and early and you can have him for the whole day,' they say. And they really, truly believe they are doing you a favour.

How does the new grandmother cope? With some difficulty, if the ones I know are anything to go by. They seek reassurance that it's perfectly OK, when they've got a desk piled with urgent correspondence and six people coming to dinner, to say: 'I'm really sorry, I'm afraid I can't have the children today.' They want sound advice on where to go/what to do/how to amuse a clutch of grandchildren (and sometimes, oh horror, their little friends). They are eager to be educated in subtle ways of getting their views across about slack discipline to a child who has never heard the word 'No'.

Would you, for instance, know how to stop your three-year-old granddaughter jumping up and down on your polished coffee table in her brand new grown-up shoes, without screaming: 'Get off that table immediately!' and for ever alienating her admiring parents ('Oh look, granny, she's dancing for you')?

Read on . . .

Kathy Jager Speaks

Kathy Jager is the fifty-seven-year-old grandmother from Phoenix, Arizona who set two world records at the World Veterans' Athletics Championship. Her incredulous Australian rivals refused to believe that a granny could clock 13.55 seconds in the 100 metres and accused her of being a man. She passed the sex test but recently had her medals withdrawn after testing positive for steroids. Kathy, a fervent anti-drugs campaigner and committed Christian, insists this is the result of the medicine she has to take for a hormonal imbalance. ('Oh ma, we can't let you go anywhere without you getting into trouble,' said daughter Tamara.) Kathy is married with two children and four grandchildren, aged from one to five.

I like to get down on the grass and play with the grandchildren, help them do handstands and fun things like that. It's not about giving them presents all the time. Benjamin, the oldest, probably realises

1

that grandma is a media star because a TV station came out to film me when he was staying with us. They were photographing me pole-vaulting and when the film came out they'd captured Benjamin running along behind me, pretending to pole-vault. I spoke to him on the telephone a few months later and he said, 'Hey, let's go and do that again, grandma, it was good fun.'

The important thing is to encourage all sides of the child. The singing and the acting, as well as the athletics. Make them well rounded.

It's wonderful to have the chance to do it all again because I didn't have time when my own two children were young, being so busy caring for them and for the house and earning money as an Avon lady to pay the college fees and so on.

"...I'M BETWEEN STEREOTYPES AT THE MOMENT..."

1
About Bonding

Not every new grandmother, gazing at her first grandchild, is instantly suffused with a 'this-is-what-life-is-all-about' glow of recognition. Some grandmothers – particularly those unwisely dressed in silk or suede – have even admitted that their only feeling, on being passed the precious bundle for the first time, was one of anxiety that the baby was dry and freshly laundered.

Others do not feel the need to claim a stake in the future through their grandchildren because they are doing it perfectly well by themselves. Lauren Bacall, seventy-five years old and still a Broadway star, is grandmother of five. 'Not a very good one,' she said recently. 'I've said to my kids, "I'm not up for baby-sitting. I sat through three kids of my own and that was quite enough."'

Leslie Kenton appears to be equally busy and un-besotted. She won fame as a health guru and was the first beauty editor to suggest that a healthy diet was a better beauty aid than a face pack. She wrote books, novels, became a photographer (her next book features herbs in exquisite close-up) and she's just finished a master class on directing and is planning her first feature film. She has four children; the oldest, Branton, is forty, the youngest, Aaron, is eighteen. I spoke to her in New Zealand where she was holding seminars on expanding consciousness and visiting Branton, his Cambodian wife and their one-year-old son, Attica, Leslie's first grandchild.

'When I was told I was going to be a grandmother I was totally indifferent,' she said. 'Couldn't care less. People said. 'Just you wait, you'll feel differently when the baby is born.' Well, I don't. I was pregnant when I was seventeen and I've been looking after children, doing jobs I didn't always want to do to pay the rent, for forty years. I have loved motherhood more than anything else I've done and if my children want to have children, that's fine, but don't include me. For the first time in my life I'm free to do my own work. I'm asking myself, what do I want to do with my life? Most people ask themselves that at eighteen. I'm starting at fifty-eight.'

Having said all that, and stressing how respectful her children are of her attitude, Leslie went on to tell me that from the moment Attica was born, if he was crying or a bit out of sorts, all she had to do was hold him and he was fine. 'There does seem to be some sort of connection. I'm Leslie. He's Attica. Just two human beings, not grandmother and grandchild, but there is definitely a link.'

I said she sounded just like a grandmother. Really, it's nothing less than a miracle the way a baby can win over an insouciant granny and begin the bonding process. Just a half-smile and the grip of tiny fingers and the most unwilling grandmother will soon have a boasting book full of photographs.

Journalist Ruth Gorb, a devoted grandmother of two, feels it's not so much a matter of wanting to become a grandmother, more a matter of needing. 'It's very primitive and probably has to do with the genes and keeping the race going,' she says, 'and when the grandchildren arrive it's a passionate relationship. Like falling in love. You can't wait to see them, you're miserable when they go and you think of them all the time.'

You'll know when the bonding process begins. It happens when the first well-meaning friend looks in the pram and is reminded vividly of one of the in-laws. 'He's got Gerald's nose. Had you noticed?'

Since what you've been noticing, from day one, is

the astonishing resemblance between your grandson's nose and the nose you see reflected in the mirror each morning, you will be surprised to find yourself choked by a rush of unfamiliar emotions, involving words like 'primordial', 'primeval' and 'proprietorial'.

You'll know you're bonding when remarks made by the little one, which you would have previously considered unappealingly cute, seem really rather endearing, if not unusually perspicacious and intelligent. Since most grandmothers, talking about their grandchildren, could bring a tired glaze to the eye of the Ancient Mariner, it's an intimidating thought that in the States you can visit a web site entitled 'alt.discussmygrandchild' and exchange competitive tales. And yet I know that if it were possible for me to tap into this group of thirty thousand or so gossiping grans, I'd be as keen as the rest of them to recount yet again my favourite granddaughter story. It was the occasion when Maudie, aged two and a half, was asked by her father if she'd like to go to the office with him. She looked at him thoughtfully for a moment and then said, with a casual toss of the head, 'Hmm . . . nice idea.' Suddenly I could see the point of grandchildren.

Anna Haycraft (the novelist Alice Thomas Ellis), says that although she's never been one for looking in prams and wouldn't think of deliberately seeking out the company of a child, she remembers vividly a bonding moment with Joshua, her first grandchild. 'He was walking down the stairs and I looked up and said to him, "Oh, I do love you, little Josh", to which he surprised me with, "What does love mean? It means not being lost, doesn't it?" Well, I think that's pretty profound for a three-year-old, don't you?'

Another bonding sign is when you start worrying. You think you've got through all the ties and troubles of childcare and then there's this disturbing tug which stops you taking off for three months in Cuba or buying a vineyard in the South of France. Shouldn't Chloe be speaking properly by now? Why are they sending Thomas to that dreadful school? Is the baby-sitter mad, like those child-shaking nannies you keep reading about in the papers?

A friend of ours, alarmed by the fact that her delight-ful four-year-old granddaughter couldn't string two words together, found it impossible to broach the subject with her son and daughter-in-law. Naturally, she couldn't come right out and ask if they thought something was wrong with Jemma, because that would be interfering and she knew that grandmothers must never commit this ultimate sin.

Sometimes she tried nudging the subject into the conversation. Like: 'Is Jemma getting on all right at school?'

'What do you mean, "Is she getting on all right at school?" her son or daughter-in-law would reply challengingly. 'Why shouldn't she be?'

Eventually, my friend splashed out on a party, which she rightly considered a bit more subtle than an intimate lunch or dinner, as she'd cunningly included in the group an old friend who happened to be a speech therapist, as well as her son and daughter-in-law. They were still on the first round of drinks when she spotted her son (obviously more worried than he'd let on) chatting up the speech therapist. Jemma started special lessons a few weeks later. Two years on she still isn't a great chatterer but at least she can communicate. And she no longer gets teased by her horrid little peers at school.

There's a belief about that it's harder nowadays for grandparents and grandchildren to get together and form any kind of real attachment. We look back to a sepia past which never really existed, and sigh for the good old days when families lived close to each other, providing a loving support network. And if the children ran around the corner to cosy old nan's house she would be waiting for them, griddle scones on the range, oil lamp at the ready, storybook in hand.

It's a myth. Back in the early 1900s, if there was a nan living around the corner she may well have looked old, from coping with washing and scrubbing without white goods or electric light, not to mention all that griddling and mucky range-care, but she was probably under fifty since life expectancy for most women in those days was around forty-eight.

Today's grandparents see more of their grand-children than any previous generation. They have to. When mother and father are both out working, who is regularly left holding the baby? When I called on Anna Haycraft she was on the phone: 'No, I really can't, sweetheart,' she was saying. 'I'm so sorry. I've got to go out to this wretched lunch. No ... Oh, I am sorry. Well, you'll just have to shelve it for today ... make up for it tomorrow. Oh dear ... well, I'll ring you the minute I get back and you can bring him round.'

'Your daughter?' I asked.

'My son-in-law,' she replied.

Isaac, aged twenty months, comes round to Anna's house most days and his high-chair is a fixture at the kitchen table alongside the manuscript of her latest book. How does she find the time to write? 'One seizes the moment,' she says.

It's easier to keep in touch these days, too. The over-fifties have far higher levels of disposable cash than their parents and grandparents ever had. It would have taken granny in her shawl eight hours to travel from York to London up the A1, but an agile, affluent fifty-year-old can jump on a jet in New York and be in London in almost half that time. A recent report from Age Concern confirms this, stating that two-thirds of today's grandparents are more involved in the lives of their grandchildren than their parents ever were with their grandchildren.

You don't even have to get on a plane or a bus to bond. Kathy Jager, the fifty-seven-year-old granny from Phoenix, Arizona, who sprints along the race track to rapturous cries of, 'Keep running, granny', talks regularly to her four grandchildren every week or so. 'It's a good way of keeping in touch,' she told me. 'Benjamin is five and very verbal. We can have real conversations about what he's doing and how he's doing. I do send them things, like a book, maybe. They like the idea that there's something in the mail addressed to them personally. They say, "Ooh, it must be from grandma." ' She chuckles in a fond, grandmotherly sort of way. 'Well, of course it is. No-body else ever sends them anything.'

And had you ever considered e-mailing a toddler? Another bonding agent that was unavailable to granny in the shawl. 'Did you know that Jan regularly e-mails her five-year-old grandson?' I marvelled to a friend recently. 'That's nothing,' she replied competitively. 'Edward and I have been e-mailing each other since he was three.'

She assures me that if you've got the modem in your computer there's nothing easier. The service is supplied free, the cost is a standard local telephone charge and all you have to do is type in your message, press SEND and make sure your grandchild is down-loading at the other end.

The Negroponte Media Lab in Boston did a study to see who used e-mail the most. Was it businessmen? Computer nerds? Academics? No. It was grandparents and grandchildren talking to each other.

I think it was Freud who, when he wasn't thinking about sex, came up with the idea that the strongest bonding agent between grandparents and grand-children is the sharing of a mutual enemy, or as Sally Greengross of Age Concern once remarked more kindly and much more tactfully, 'One of the best aspects for me is the conspiracies. We are allies against the parents.'

Novelist Beryl Bainbridge would probably agree with that. She has six grandchildren and in an article in *You* magazine she told Catherine O'Brien:

> They have their own room here – a toy room which they also sleep in. I have lots of toy guns, which their parents don't approve of, but which I allow them to have. The little ones have chocolate biscuits which their parents don't have at home, and the older ones watch television, which is restricted when they are with their parents.

And Anna Haycraft, describing her relationship with Isaac, says: 'I'm his accomplice. When he wants to do something mummy and daddy don't want he takes my hand and leads me to whatever naughtiness he wants to do and implicates me. I'm the one who lets him play with water. He splashes everywhere in here which couldn't matter less and he wraps himself in wet towels and does a funny walk. He makes me laugh.'

Ruth Westheimer Speaks

Dr Ruth Westheimer, the psychosexual therapist and co-author of *Grandparenthood*,* has three grandchildren, aged eight to eleven, and says she was so pleased at becoming a grandmother that she stopped dyeing her hair.

You need to be very careful offering advice. Just because you did things a certain way doesn't mean it's the only right way. Most new parents, especially those with a first child, are already anxious, confused and exhausted. With little or no experience of a small baby to fall back upon, new parents worry when the baby cries or is quiet for too long. Many women are particularly anxious about breastfeeding, especially at the beginning. What they need from you more

*Routledge, 1998.

than anything else is reassurance, support, and, on occasion, some relief. Maybe it has been too long and you don't remember how overwhelming it can be to be totally responsible for a little human life for the first time. But, if you think back, you will probably recall how important it was to you to know that you were doing a good job. The more confident and secure your grandchild's parents feel, the easier it will be for them to pass those feelings on to their child.

"DON'T YOU LOVE THE POP-UP DINOSAUR?"

2

Naming Names

John Travolta has decided to call his new-born baby Spam because his wife, Kelly Preston, craved this reconstituted meat treat during her pregnancy and kept a tin in the bedroom. Their son is named Jett, after Travolta's love of flying.

I'd no sooner stopped brooding over the bleak future of young Spam than I read about the pun-loving mother in Bath who named her first child Obvious and her second son Shaw. Obvious-Lee and Shaw-Lee. No doubt the mother cracks up every time she introduces her children to a stranger but I don't suppose Obvious and Shaw laugh a lot. The mother says that Ovvy's classmates think that his name is cool.

There's not much you can do about the ghastly names your children give your grandchildren, but one suspects that by labelling their little ones Spam or Fifi Trixiebelle or with a jokey pun the parents are making a bid to be different.

If I were Mrs Travolta snr or Mrs Preston, for that matter, I'd greet the news with a cry of pleasure. 'What a lovely idea. And what a coincidence.' And naming the close friend my son and daughter-in-law particularly disliked and despised for being boringly bourgeois, I'd add: 'Jane has just been on the phone, to tell me that her daughter has had a baby and they're calling him Spam, too.'

Friends of ours phoned recently in some distress. Their new grandchild was to be named Jesus. They agreed that it was an appropriate name for a little boy destined to be a major religious prophet, and perfectly acceptable if he happened to live in Mexico City or Havana, but considered it grimly character-forming for their grandson whose name had been put down already for a traditional English public school. My friends bemoaned the fact that they couldn't even think of a suitable diminutive, so they try to call him nothing at all. 'How's the boy doing?' they say.

We have no control over our grandchildren's names,

but we can have a try at getting our own names right. Gran? Nan? Phyllis? Like being asked to produce your bus pass when you've requested a concession at the cinema, it's all right if people rear back, amazed by your unlikely maturity, but are you ready to be labelled Grandmother, aka Senior Citizen?

Joy Matthews has always been Joy to her grandchildren. She was thirty-seven, the fashion editor of a national newspaper, when she became a grandmother for the first time. 'I was at a party, dancing with an extremely attractive man when a woman, who ceased at that moment to be my friend, called out: "Joy . . . darling. How's your dear little grandchild?" '

The consensus seems to be that Grandma is acceptable, if a trifle austere and Granny is OK; nobody wants to be known as Nan or Gran, thank you very much. Writing about this in the *Sunday Times* from the male viewpoint, Professor Laurie Taylor remembered assuring his son that of course he was pleased that he was going to have a grandchild but wouldn't it make matters easier if they could somehow get rid of words like Grandad, Grandfather and especially Gramps? Couldn't the child simply know him as Laurie until it reached an age when it could understand the nature of their relationship? Or was there some other term?

It turned out that there was. His ex-wife, thrilled about her new role had, nevertheless, drawn the line at becoming Grandma or Granny and had decided she'd like to be referred to by a phrase she'd come across in the States, Second Generation Parent. It hardly seemed a homely term of endearment and Laurie imagined his new little grandchild playing happily in the garden when all of a sudden the french windows would be thrown open and daddy would call out, 'Darling, look who's come to see you. It's your Second Generation Parent.'

Evidently she has stuck to this title and Laurie's son said that only the other day the boy, now five years old, had become upset at the fact that his grandmother was reading a novel rather than taking her proper place in goal. Looking up at his dad he had said, with great earnestness, 'She's not a very good Second Generation Parent, is she?'

New parents are, on the whole, very courteous about asking you what you'd like to be called. We had a serious family sit-down on the subject. There were two Grannies already. Did I want to be the third Granny? Would Step-Granny be more appropriate? How about just Shirley? I said just Shirley would be fine but this was a pretty pointless discussion since the new mother (my step-daughter) and her sister and brother, invited to call me Shirley, had invariably referred to me, affectionately I like to think, by nicknames on the lines of 'bat-lugs' or 'dumbo'. I could see no reason why their children would grow up to be any more respectful.

Two sets of grandparents who minded terribly

what they were called, and thought it would be more youth-enhancing to be known as Miranda and Jeremy and Ros and Brian, were adamant that they were not going to put up with any silly pet names. Miranda and Jeremy are now called Granny and Grandpa Seaside because they live in Brighton, and the other couple answer moodily to the names Den-Den (Ros) and Bigger Den-Den (Brian) for some reason known only to their grandchildren.

Columnist Katharine Whitehorn recommends leaving it to the baby to choose the name. 'You start with Granny and Grandpa, or whatever, and they take it from there. My mother was always called Danny by our two sons and then Danny by all of us. The attempt at my name came out as Baff, and now I'm Baff to all the family.'

Actress Prunella Scales is an unlikely Grandma Beard. This is because she is married to Grandpa Beard. When their two grandchildren were getting around to calling them anything at all, Prunella's husband, Timothy West, was playing Falstaff and sporting a splendid beard. Now he's in Ibsen with a moustache and Prunella is pleased they do not call her Grandma Tache.

She has pointed out to him that as he was a grandfather at forty-one when Juliet (the daughter from his first marriage) had her first daughter, Kate, and as Kate was now nineteen it was quite possible that she could get married and have a baby, thus making him a great-grandfather. Timothy took the Gorbachev line on this (Gorby: 'Did you ever think you'd get to sleep with the President?' Raisa: 'Did *you* ever think you'd sleep with the President's wife?') and said he was happy about becoming a great-grandfather but didn't much like the idea of being the father of a grandmother.

The thing to bear in mind is that small children learn like parrots and will latch onto words if they are repeated often enough. If you really want to be known by your Christian name, label your presents in capital letters, 'with lots of love from SUSAN', announce yourself as Susan on the telephone, pretend you can't hear them when they call you anything other than Susan.

And, having said that, the grandchildren will probably go right ahead and call you what they were going to call you, anyway.

Angela Flowers Speaks

Angela Flowers, art dealer and chair of Flowers East Gallery, has five children and nine grandchildren.

I love it when the grandchildren rush through the door into my arms, I love that, but I'm afraid out of sight is out of mind. My children think I'm a rotten grandmother but they thought I was a rotten mother, too. There was always that accusatory tone, You weren't there at the speech day, or whatever and, of course, I was. They've got this selective memory.

I remember my own grandmother saying, 'Is there anything you'd like to talk about?' and that was wonderful, because you can't talk to your parents, can you? I try and do that. Actually, my relationship with my grandchildren is much easier than my relationship with my own children.

A couple of years ago I took Patrick, who was

then ten, to lunch at the Ivy. He still talks about it. The maitre'd said: 'Oh, what are you going to see?' and I said, 'We're not going to see anything. We're just having lunch.'

IT'S A DIAMANTE BABY SLING
DEAR, FOR EVENING WEAR ...

3

Culture Shock

It's all so different, isn't it? For a start, you're lucky if, when your daughter announces she's going to have a baby, she has already been through the process of a marriage ceremony. At several recent weddings the skill of the designer was not so much to present the bride at her glowing best, but to puffball the skirt appealingly below the bodice to conceal the bulge. At one wedding several middle-aged ladies tsk-ed disapprovingly under their hats as the bride (in white) and groom were followed down the aisle by their two-year-old son, dressed as a tiny pageboy. And the vicar, nodding amiably in the child's direction, gave thanks 'for the blessing of Jonathan, the fruit of their union'.

Not that we need to be told when a modern mum is expecting. Following the full frontal nakedness of Demi Moore exposing her fecundity, the fashion is not to conceal but to flaunt. Like Posh Spice's pregnant party-gear, the maternity dress is not an A-line flowing sort of garment but skin-tight Lycra. The Gap is also popular, where a short cardigan (the bottom three buttons undone) doesn't meet the low-slung mini-skirt or trousers below.

A friend of mine had a call from her mother the other day. Her pregnant granddaughter had been staying with her and there had been a significant absence of maternity clothes. 'There has been a maximum display of your daughter's tummy in Norfolk this week,' she told my friend.

You must, of course, say nothing except, perhaps, 'What a pretty cardigan', and this will be excellent practice for all the future culture shocks which should have you biting your lip.

Breastfeeding, for instance. You've no sooner come to terms with the visible pregnancy than you're faced with the naked breast. Some of us find it perfectly charming and natural to breastfeed the baby over lunch in Café Rouge or in the middle of Harrods but there are others who are mildly embarrassed and can't see why the young mother couldn't have fed the baby before she came out or, at least, behind the dressing gowns in Lingerie rather than in the centre of Evening and Occasional Wear.

How do you call a halt to this without sounding like a puritanical old fuddy-duddy? If you'd been the mother of that Russian chess-player who threatened to whip out a breast and feed her baby during the championship game, for instance, you'd probably have had lots of good advice for your daughter. Like, 'For God's sake, Ludmilla, leave the baby at home.' Or, 'You'll only upset daddy.' It is hardly necessary to add that Ludmilla would not have valued her mother's advice on this subject, or on any other subject, for that matter.

There are subtler ways to get your views across. Ludmilla's mother would have been wise to dwell thoughtfully on the high stress levels at international chess tournaments while quoting the current child expert's view (and they always have one) about the adverse effect tension has on both breast-milk and baby. If she'd then offered to stay at home with bottle and grandchild she'd have been labelled a star rather than an old-fashioned busybody.

Mealtimes, as ever, are another bone of contention between the generations. 'We had meals at set times and the children had to sit down and eat up until they had finished,' a grandmother of four children between the ages of two and six says, with pursed lips. 'This lot eat with their hands – particularly revolting with pasta, which they adore – and they are up and down, messing about, throughout the meal.'

This is a common complaint from grandparents and the answer is to anchor the toddler to the table in one of those clip-on high-chairs. They don't come cheap, but it's a small price to pay for not having your grandchild jump on the table, tear off her clothes, and nick the ham from your plate while the parents beam approvingly. If they are too old for high-chair restraint, adjust your eating hours accordingly. When you're told that the children will be staying up to supper, or joining you for lunch, it would be unwise to say, 'But it's well past their bedtime . . .' or 'Shouldn't they be having their rest . . . ?' The most efficient way to activate the parents into the kitchen is to say, 'Oh, how lovely. But I'm afraid it won't be ready for an hour and a half.'

It's difficult, sometimes, to come to terms with such modern child-rearing methods as 'food on demand' and 'take-it-as-it-comes' toilet training, but there's sense in spooning food into a child's mouth when he's hungry rather than have him spit it out to your timetable. And having a 'clean' baby at three months, a familiar nanny boast in our day, is only practical if there's a nanny around or a mother with time on her hands, since it's not the baby but the adult who becomes trained to change the nappy or fetch the potty at the vital moment.

What happens, though, if your grandchild is still wandering around in nappies at the age of two and a half? One grandmother I know began to wonder if her granddaughter was going to be the first girl in England to go straight from Pampers to Tampax. 'My son and daughter-in-law are great admirers of all things Third World,' she says, 'and consider it perfectly natural for the child to defecate where she pleases and when she feels like it. What they don't realise is that this bodily function only functions regularly if you stick to a routine.' When the parents went away she offered to look after the grandchild. 'I had her potty-trained in two weeks,' she says proudly.

The other major bone of contention between the generations is the dummy. In one decade it's A Bad Thing because it deforms the jaw, in the next it's A Good Thing because it encourages the baby to suck. Currently, it's A Good Thing. 'I was horrified the first time I saw my daughter-in-law plug a dummy into the baby's mouth,' says one grandmother, 'and then I saw the sense of it. A dummy has to be better than the baby sucking her thumb. You can get rid of the dummy but you can't get rid of the thumb.'

Gradually, most of us learn to accept the ever-changing fashions in childcare, but what we do find hard to understand is the togetherness thing. A grandmother-to-be was shopping in Mothercare for tiny jackets and bibs when a pretty young girl queued up behind her at the cash desk, carrying a bag of shopping and with her baby in a sling on her bosom. The baby threw up all over her and all over the shopping. The grandmother-to-be dodged smartly sideways. 'I can't think of anything worse than carrying my baby around on my person,' she said. 'I'm for four-hourly feeds, putting the baby in the pram and wheeling it down to the other end of the garden.

'I told my daughter this and she responded by buying her own sling and announcing that she was intending to sleep with the baby in her bed. "Whatever for?" I said. "He needs to feel protected," she said.'

Console yourself with the thought that sleeping *en famille* is an accepted practice all over the world. Evidently they do it a lot in Guatemala and judging by the number of Guatemalans singing and strumming instruments in tourist squares around the world, they have not all been smothered in bed by their sleeping parents, as we grandparents secretly fear will happen to our own grandchildren.

We've got friends who have not only shared their bed with their two young daughters from birth but won't be separated from them for a second. People are always asking them impertinently how they managed to conceive the second child and they always reply that they did it in the usual way. When they go out they take the children with them. They even teach them at home.

'Why not leave them with the in-laws if you don't trust hired help?' I suggested.

'That would be even worse,' they said darkly, and if we didn't know their parents we'd have imagined that they had been the subject of the most appalling child abuse. It turned out that they were keen to avoid the grandparents having any influence over the two girls, since they had made their disapproval of the way they were being brought up all too clear. Another case where it would have been wiser to hold the tongue and bite the lip.

As the children grew up, we wiser, older friends and relatives shook our heads sadly at the lack of social graces and academic skills they would undoubtedly have, but happily (and irritatingly) they have turned out well adjusted, polite, chatty, clever and pretty, too. 'Perhaps we did it all wrong, after all,' one of the grandmothers said sadly.

But what shocks grandparents most about all this excessive bonding is the cash outlay. If you invite your children out to a family lunch you can be sure that they will bring the grandchildren, too. And that includes the toddler and the baby. And if, like kind friends of mine, you offer to take the whole family skiing, you may find, as they did, that their daughter and son-in-law will refuse to leave the two-year-old at home. Cost? An extra £500 for the non-skier.

In our day (as we grandmothers say) a children's party meant tea with tiny sandwiches, sausages and a cake, a few rousing games, usually involving tears when child (a) hit child (b) or child (c) was accused by the others of pushing and Not Being Fair, followed by a clutch of balloons and home at five thirty with a bag of Smarties.

Now it's off to the theatre to see *Peter Pan* or a panto in a hired limo, or £70-plus for a two-hours'

takeover at the local swimming pool, or an extrava-
ganza at home involving the hire of small tables and
chairs and tents. Have you ordered the Bouncy
Castle? No party is complete without one. Have you
booked the entertainer? Children expect a first-rate
performance of magic, tricks and stories where they
are encouraged to participate and show off. Incidentally, the current crop of entertainers are often so
camp they make Julian Clary seem robustly macho.
A youthful and sophisticated granny reports that at
her three-year-old granddaughter's party one such
entertainer, who had a false bum attached amusingly
to his rear, turned around and mooned at the children.
'The infants loved it, of course,' she said, 'and the
mothers didn't notice because they were all so besot-
ted at seeing their young socialising, but I couldn't
stop myself clapping my hand to my mouth in
horror.'

And then there's the leaving gift – something
unusual and expensive for each child which won't
shame the small host or hostess. 'We got videos at
Sarah's party,' a four-year-old remarked, listlessly un-
wrapping a mini-book.

The word 'spoilt' is often used when grandmothers get together and compare notes about all
the unsuitable things their grandchildren are allowed
to do. They are allowed to stay up until all hours,
they are allowed to dress up like little grown-ups in
designer gear and jig about to pop music, they are
allowed to slump in front of television or the computer

instead of running about in the fresh air, their rooms are full of bright, plastic toys when ours used to play with cardboard boxes – hold on, a minute. Did *your* child play happily with cardboard boxes? Mine only ever dismantled a cardboard box when he was searching eagerly for the gift inside it. Grandmothers, too, suffer from selective memory syndrome.

Anna Haycraft Speaks

Anna Haycraft, the novelist and columnist Alice Thomas Ellis, has five children and six grandchildren.

I was still being a mother when I became a grandmother. Sarah, my youngest, became an auntie at twelve. 'When can I have a baby?' she kept saying. Oliver, the father, was only twenty-four, which is young, as you know they don't grow up these days until they're about forty.

Josh, my oldest grandchild, is at Ampleforth and his parents live in California, so I have to go and watch rugby and stuff which I must say is a terrible shock. I thought all that was behind me. Isaac spends a lot of time here because both his mummy and daddy are working. Charlotte goes to school around the corner and is about to do her Common Entrance, so we're going to work on her essays together.

I see myself as a backstop. Any emergency and

33

I'll drop everything else and put them at the top of my list. It's a flaming nuisance but there it is. That's family.

'IT'S A CRÈCHE FOR GRANDMOTHERS'...

4

The Fatigue Factor

You love your grandchildren, of course you do, but children are noisy and feckless and on the go from dawn's first flush until they are eventually coerced into cot or bed at least an hour after you'd planned on sitting down to dinner with a glass of wine. They are exhausting, which is why it's such a good idea for people to have babies when they are young, and why women who think nothing of swimming fifty lengths before breakfast, and emerge bright-eyed from an all-day board meeting, find it necessary to retire to bed

35

with an aspirin when they've spent an afternoon with their grandchildren.

Even Oprah Winfrey, a woman who had no trouble at all controlling a studio full of serial murderers, met her match when she was left with her goddaughter for four hours. 'I was *so* worn out,' she said, '*so* exhausted, and *so* grateful to her mother for coming back.'

'I feel desperately miserable when I don't see enough of my two grandchildren and totally exhausted when I do,' says one grandmother. 'What you have to bear in mind is the weight. It's all very well when he's a dear little baby, but when he's eighteen months and says, "Carry me, granny", your back gives out.

'I had them for the weekend when their parents went away and I was absolutely on my knees and dying for a whisky by their bedtime. They love running up and down the stairs and falling down them, too. You have to watch them all the time and take them to the park and the zoo and by the time you've fed them and got them into bed you've had it.'

In her book, *Grandparenthood*, Dr Ruth Westheimer has a daunting list of sixteen things which you should do to childproof your house before letting a child loose in it. These include getting on the floor to check for coins, nuts or buttons the child might choke on, covering your electric sockets with plastic covers and putting practically everything you normally leave on tables onto a high shelf. In the circumstances you may consider conserving your energy by going round to the parents' house to look after the grand-children.

One grandmother who fell foul of Dr Ruth's thirteenth rule (remove all keys from door locks), says she wishes she'd gone out to do the caring instead of having them round to her house when the two granddaughters, aged three and four, somehow managed to lock the bathroom door on themselves. 'The key was still in the lock outside so we pushed it under the door, and relying on the natural competitiveness of children, said things like, "Who's the cleverest girl?" and "There's a prize waiting for the one who opens the door first." They took no notice because they'd got into my make-up bag and were covering themselves and the bathroom in creams and lipstick.'

The children emerged eventually and the grand-mother suggested that Dr Ruth might add a seventeenth rule, 'Keep your cosmetics out of sight.' 'It didn't harm the children,' she said, 'but it cost me a fortune in Clarins.'

'The idea that your children are off your hands at eighteen is just nonsense,' said a tired grandmother of six. 'The moment they've got children of their own you're on permanent standby. One day they're on the phone saying, "Don't come round this afternoon, so-and-so is going to be there and you'll only say something embarrassing." And then next day the phone rings and it's, "I'm working today and the au pair's sick. Can you possibly hold the fort? Oh, and ask dad if he can collect Sam from James Simmond's birthday party and he's got to be there at four on the dot." '

An indomitable Scottish great-granny of 101 – she gave up her job last year because she thought it was inappropriate for a woman of 100 to run an old people's charity – reports that all her young friends at the bridge club have some sort of regular commitment to grandchildren. 'You see pensioners pushing prams all over high streets and parks,' she says. 'It's the one-parent families they have these days. And so many clever girls keep on their careers and don't have babies until the very last minute. Which, of course, makes for older grannies as well as older mothers.'

Today's generation of grandparents are more than twice as likely to act as childminders to their grand-children than their parents, but not all these loyal pram-pushers are childminding while mother goes out to work. An increasing number have, for one reason or another, been left holding the baby and, in many cases, a whole raft of grandchildren. No empty nest, no nest egg, either. In these families it's trainers for the teenagers instead of cream teas or G and Ts for grandma and grandpa.

I came across an interesting page in the *Guardian* recently about two different groups of these put-upon grandmothers. One article revealed that in the last five years five thousand Jamaicans, mainly of retirement age, have gone quietly home. Eugenie Bryan, a Jamaican mother who wrote the article, says that within her circle of friends she is one of the few still to have Jamaican-born grandparents in this country. Her children's paternal grandparents have gone and hers are returning soon 'to live in the sun among mango trees and hummingbirds'. It's a tradition in the Caribbean for the young father to bunk off, leaving mother to work and grandma to look after the children (often bringing them up with her own) and in Britain, black families have a one-in-three chance of being brought up by a single parent. So what, Eugenie wonders, is to become of these children left without the matriarch, the linchpin of an extended family? 'It is in interacting across the generations that culture is passed down the bloodline and where social skills are learned. This is where the future looks bleak for Britons.'

The second article revealed another disturbing trend: the growing band of grandparents who are having to bring up children the second time around. Of course grandma has always stepped in when a mother dies or is physically or mentally incapable of looking after her children, but now we have to add to that the increase in teenage pregnancy and the breakdown of families and, most of all, the Children Act of 1989 which, instead of putting children into care or with foster parents or up for adoption, encourages the courts to keep children in the family, 'so long as the grandparents or other relatives can do it'.

Journalist Jeanne Davis, visiting a support group of these second-time-around parents while researching the article, found that they had unique problems. How do you explain to a six-year-old why your mother or father doesn't want you or is unable to keep you? What intricacies of logic do you search for to explain to two adolescents that daddy really does care for them even though he chose a second marriage and the stepchildren that came with it? The answer, as most grandparents would guess, is to give them even more love and kisses and cuddles than you gave your own children at a similar age.

This group of grandparents will not be going to live among mango trees and hummingbirds. Where are they going? According to Jeanne Davis, back to school to grasp the new maths and to master computer technology so that they can help with the homework.

Grandmothers who feel they've been there, done that, and it's their turn now to sit back and do nothing very much, will no doubt have been discouraged to hear about the government's rent-a-granny scheme which is already in action in Essex. Mothers with small children who do not have close relatives to help out can apply for community grandmothers. 'It will be like recreating an extended family,' said a Department for Education and Employment spokesperson hopefully. 'When a person is feeling low, they have someone to turn to.'

It sounds like baby-sitting on the cheap to me. And the government's other proposal, to pay grandmothers £100 a week to look after their grandchildren, is another non-starter, according to Professor Dench from the Institute of Community Studies, who has been researching the subject. 'Grandparents have their own lives to lead,' he says. 'Many of them are still working and – even though they love their grandchildren dearly – simply don't want to take on the main responsibilities of parenting.'

'My children are always ringing up saying how they'd love to come and see me, and then they arrive, dump the children on me and go off and do their own thing,' a grandmother told me recently. 'I had four children of my own and I wonder how I ever cooked meals and worked at a paid job. I suppose it's because when they're yours you can leave them to scream, but when they're not yours you feel you have to keep checking on them every second.'

She devised schemes to keep them occupied. Very young children like doing grown-up things, so she said, 'I need a helper with the washing up. Any offers?' and she covered the kitchen floor with towels and let the three grandchildren stand at the sink squirting Fairy Liquid at a set of saucepans and plastic utensils. Older children, needless to say, know all about washing up and how to avoid it and will not be eager to join in this game.

'My lot love cooking – well, messing about with food,' she says. 'I make a batch of dough before they arrive, provide piles of currants and nuts and colourful things like Smarties and let them get on with it. What they actually do, of course, is eat the Smarties, but it keeps them busy for at least half an hour.'

She also keeps a small patch of garden, discreetly

concealed behind a shed, where the children can dig and plant seeds and throw mud at each other, and when it's warm enough fills an old zinc bath with water so they can splash about, float boats and ducks and chuck water as well as mud.

'Children love sploshing about with paint,' she says, 'but they're always given rotten little paint brushes that don't work, so I set up an easel in the garden and let them use my proper brushes and paints.'

The resulting artwork was so good that she framed one of the pictures. But that just might have been because she's a grandmother.

Grandmothers are meant to be able to do grand-motherly things like sing nursery rhymes, dance the polka, make paper aeroplanes and rag dolls, mend broken toys and bake birthday cakes that look like engines or teddy bears. Forget it. You won't have the energy for any of these taxing pastimes. Children chatter incessantly and the easiest way to entertain them is to listen, giving them your full attention. Parents don't have much time for that.

There was a story in the newspapers a while back about a three-year-old who popped into the kitchen to tell his mother, busy with the washing, that he was going to see granny. 'That's nice, dear,' she said, without looking up from her sheet-folding. Granny lived in Basingstoke and an hour or so later a police car picked up the small boy pedalling eagerly along the M3 in his toy car and returned him to his distraught mother.

The most comforting thing about being a grand-mother (or, indeed, a godmother like Oprah), is that at the end of the day somebody will come and collect the grandchildren and you can wave them goodbye.

'Do you remember the aunt in *Just William* who remarked that now he had left she began to quite like William?' says Anna Haycraft. 'Well, that's me. I'm a hermit, rather fond of being alone. The other day I had this simply wonderful feeling and couldn't think why and then I realised that I was absolutely alone and it was bliss.'

Penny Vincenzi Speaks

Penny Vincenzi, the novelist, and her husband Paul, have four daughters and four grandchildren, two boys and two girls aged between one and five.

Mothers today have right on their side. I look back incredulously at the beleaguered person who had to change her babies' nappies in public lavatories, whose humble requests to have bottles warmed in cafes and motorway service stations were greeted with derision or refusal, who had to lie to the office and say that she – never the baby – was ill, so fortunate was she to be entrusted with a job at all, given that she was a mother and labelled U for Unreliable. I gaze spellbound at young fathers not only feeding and changing babies, but scooping them up, unprompted, to be bathed and read to; and I can only wonder at the superb day nurseries which have replaced grisly au pairs as the support system to working mothers.

On the other hand, I could eat cheese and have a glass of wine while I was pregnant, dump the babies into a carry cot and thence onto the back seat of the car and take them to other people's houses without so much as ruffling the blankets (rather than hauling them in and out of car seats), stiffen up the six-o'clock bottle with Farex when they were a month old, thereby greatly increasing the chances of sleeping through, and administer the odd brisk slap without feeling I had condemned them to a lifetime in psychiatric care.

Technically and socially things have changed beyond all recognition, but babies have remained basically the same. In the end, the baby always wins.

"HE WAS GETTING NO EXERCISE SITTING MOTIONLESS IN FRONT OF THE TELLY, SO WE CONFISCATED THE REMOTE..."

5

Granny Instinct

One of the most pleasing aspects of becoming a grandmother is that your children, who have scarcely listened to anything you've said to them for twenty or thirty years, and have certainly ignored your advice on lovers, careers or how to do their hair, suddenly realise that they've got a childcare expert down the road, or at the other end of the phone.

A friend of mine had a visit from her daughter, her son-in-law and her new granddaughter the other day. The daughter, on maternity leave from the merchant bank where she runs a department and earns more than £100,000 a year, is clearly no fool but she arrived in tears holding her baby in a manic, protective sort of way. 'Oh, mummy,' she wept, 'I don't know what to do. The District Nurse says that Phoebe isn't on the right centile curve, she hasn't put on enough weight.'

'The right what?' her mother said, taking her glowingly healthy granddaughter in her arms and inspecting her closely. 'What a lot of nonsense. Anyone can see there's nothing wrong with this baby.'

At that moment, the new father, who had been parking the car, came in and pointed anxiously at a spot on the baby's face. 'Oh, my God, look at that!' he exclaimed. 'Phoebe's inherited my eczema.'

'That's not eczema,' said my friend. 'That's a milk spot. It'll probably be gone by morning.' And it was.

My local GP calls this granny instinct and says he is constantly surprised at the way the dizzy young women he treated when he first came into the practice have turned into sensible grannies. 'I've never known a grandmother foxed by anything,' he says. 'They have experience and knowledge of the child so presentations ring alarm bells. They remind me of the senior consultant doing his ward round who stops at one of the beds and says to the junior doctor, "This man looks poorly to me, he'll be dead by the weekend." "Oh no, sir," says the young doctor, "we're treating his stomach pains and he's improving daily." The man was, of course, dead by the weekend.

'In the same way, a granny only has to glance at her crying grandchild complaining of stomach pains to know whether he is really ill or is crying because nobody has taken any notice of him for five minutes.

'I had a phone call recently from a desperate young mother whose seven-month-old son was having a fit and she didn't know what to do. I told her to fill a bath with cold water, turn on a warm shower and dip the boy alternately into the hot and cold water. There was a pause at the other end of the phone and then she said, "That's what my mother told me to do. She's sitting here now." When I arrived at the house the baby had calmed down and the grandmother had an aura of triumph about her.'

Now, I don't say we'd all have this finely tuned granny instinct in such an emergency, but I think most of us could be trusted to identify a spot or organise a tetanus injection if the grandchild fell down on a gritty playground. And we'd recognise whooping cough from the weird 'whoop' noise, as well as most of the other infectious diseases that were around when we and our children were young. What we don't know much about are the three illnesses that seem to strike down children today and obsess their parents – asthma, allergies and absolutely anything to which you can add the word 'syndrome'.

A schools inspector tells me that she was shocked, the first time she went into a primary school, to see rows of puffers (the children's jolly name for inhalers) lined up on the shelf above the coat pegs where we

used to stow our satchels. And many of my friends'
grandchildren have puffers, too. So what has caused all
this wheezing and coughing and loss of breath, and
how would we recognise asthma?

The answer is that nobody knows for sure what
causes asthma and even doctors don't always recognise
it. In the fifties medical students were taught that 'all
that wheezes is not asthma'. Now asthma is diagnosed
without a wheeze, just with a night cough. Since it's
known that at least one in seven children may cough
at night, this has led some older doctors to query
whether the reason there is so much asthma about is
because some younger doctors over-diagnose it.

Those of us who choked on Dickensian smog in
the comparatively asthma-free days when the midwife
lit up a Capstan Full Strength as she called for the
towels and boiling water, are inclined to consider the
pollution theory a non-starter – even with the added
unpleasantness of diesel fumes. Central heating, room
vaporisers, pesticide sprays and antibiotics have all
come in for their share of blame, and some medical
research suggests that anti-asthma products are signifi-
cantly more dangerous than the illness itself.

There are a lot more allergies about these days, too.
A school doctor says that the only definite advice he
can offer on the subject of food allergies is 'Don't
make a fruit cake'. 'So many children are allergic
to nuts and they can produce the most horrendous
coughing and choking, even death. Otherwise I've
observed that children are inclined to be allergic to

cabbage or carrots or broccoli, the things they don't like. The schools can't cope with it which is why they prefer the packed lunch.'

He also cites dust mites which lurk in bedding and waft about the house as a common cause of allergy and says that the latest thinking here, as with asthma, is that air ionisers and pesticide sprays and vaporisers only make matters worse, and you'd do better thoroughly vacuuming the house and the bedding.

The most common syndrome at the moment is ADS, where the hyperactive child is unable to settle in class, or anywhere else for that matter. Those of us who are unfamiliar with 'attention deficit syndrome' tend to wonder cynically if our grandchildren are actually suffering from the more familiar, 'I don't want to go to school today' syndrome. But the most likely reason why we (and our children) rarely had ADS and our grandchildren often do, is that there were far fewer additives in our food. A significant link has been found between tartrazine (a colouring agent in sweets) and hyperactivity, so taking the grandchildren a bag of coloured sweets could be as unpopular as giving them a box of chocolates. They've actually banned red Smarties in the States. An international health commission recently pointed an accusatory finger at the radiation emitted by television sets, mobiles, computer monitors and video-game screens, and said this, too, could make children violent, lower levels of concentration and damage the memory.

The sneaking suspicion that a normally active

toddler is diagnosed as having ADS if he has a temper tantrum and hurls himself at the furniture and his exhausted parents, is given credence by the amount of Ritalin (a calming medicine for hyperactive children) currently being prescribed here and in America. A pharmacist working in Sussex tells me that there is an estate near her where one child was prescribed Ritalin by a local psychiatrist, and then another and another until nearly all the children in the street were on it. 'They can't all have ADS,' she says reasonably.

When you ask a friend how the grandchildren are, she invariably sighs and says something on the lines of, 'Oh, Cordelia's got a temperature and James has an ear infection again. They're always ill. And can you be surprised when they spend hours slumped in front of the television or hunched over their computers and play stations, snacking on pizzas and baked beans. I said to my daughter, "What's the matter with fresh air and exercise and good fresh fruit and vegetables?" '

The familiar words of any mother/grandmother who Knows Best, but you could just as well be listening to a medical adviser, specialist or research scientist advising us how to prevent, ease the symptoms and even cure asthma, allergies or ADS. And you can add diabetes and obesity and ME to that list, too. What these health professionals are currently saying is that the most effective treatment for this group of illnesses is fresh air (and they consider the air fresher in a busy street than in your kitchen), plenty of exercise (good for the lungs) and a sensible diet – less fats and sugar and red meat, more fresh vegetables and fruit.

Recently scientists spent two years proving what grandmothers have known for generations, that cod liver oil is good for you. But then, so many of the articles and research papers published in the medical press sound more like old wives' tales than modern medical treatises as they extol the magic properties of such ancient herbal remedies as St John's wort for depression, valerian for sleeplessness and calendula (marigold) for soothing sore and rough skin. The ground-up root of the ginkgo biloba tree, used in the treatment of memory loss and dementia, was more prescribed by doctors in Germany during one single year than any other drug.

The words 'old wives' tales' derive from Latin by way of French and roughly translate as, 'the wise words of a woman of good repute with impeccable credentials'. Just another way of saying, granny instinct or, in the case of these particular herbal remedies, great–great–granny instinct.

Can you wonder that young parents fuss and fret over their children's health when they are bombarded daily by dire medical warnings and conflicting theories and treatments from research scientists, government health advisers and all the other official busybodies? And what makes all this advice extra worrying is that no two experts seem to agree about anything. Prozac versus St John's wort, as it were. Government health leaflets in the clinics urging mothers to scrub and sterilise every surface are countered by an influential medical research team (and any group of grannies you'd care to question) saying, 'No, no, exposure to dirt actually boosts the immune system. The reason your children keep getting sore throats is that you are keeping them and your house too clean.'

In Paris, doctors came out recently with a Mary Poppins-like notion that 'a dummy and a spoonful of sugar may be the key to soothing a baby'. Any parents intending to go out and buy a dummy and a kilo of caster sugar might well have been stopped in their tracks by another headline in the newspapers a day later announcing, 'Baby dummy ban in health alert'. Something to do with poisons in *some* of the PVC-softening agents in *some* of the soothers, as dummies are now called.

This overload of information (and don't forget you can catch hypochondria from the health sites on the internet now, too) are quite enough to make parents paranoid about the health and safety of their children without the addition of shock-horror, heavy-type headlines in the papers. 'SEX-CHANGE CHEMICALS FOUND IN BABY FOODS' and 'BEWARE THE BUG-BUSTERS' would certainly undermine my confidence if I was conscientiously feeding my baby expensive brands of baby food or buffing up my sink with a much advertised brand of disinfectant cleaner, only to read that baby's Mixed Fruit Dessert contains a cocktail of nasty drugs and the expensive anti-bacterial I am caringly spraying around the kitchen could be destroying my family's natural immune system and encouraging food poisoning.

Health professionals, rather than reassuring inexperienced parents, add to their anxieties. The bureaucratic insistence on filling in forms to deduce whether a baby is the required height, the correct weight, has the right-sized head, is eating the right food, sleeping the prescribed amount of time and swivelling his or her eyes the way they ought to be swivelling, must surely convince a new mother that if her baby focuses his eyes differently or weighs slightly less than the baby on the lap next to her at the post-natal clinic, there is something seriously wrong.

What young parents need from grandparents is not know-all advice – they've got enough of that already – but practical backup if, for instance, mother and child are stuck in hospital; somebody to look after the other children, organise the meals at home and supervise a visitors' roster. And they are keen to know that if the grandchildren come to stay in your house, there is more in the medicine chest than a collection of pill boxes with a 1970-something expiry date, a bottle of Vick and a half-empty can of hairspray. What they hope to see in there, along with all the usual first aid kit – bandages, plasters, dressings, scissors, antiseptic cream, mild cough sweets and so on – is Waspeze for anaesthetising stings, lavender oil to antagonise midges and mosquitoes, Jelonet to soothe burns instantly, Lasonil to minimise bruising, Dioralyte, a rehydration fluid for treating diarrhoea, and Calpol, a child-strength liquid paracetamol which, judging by the amount consumed, is more palatable to this generation of children than Junior Aspirin was to ours.

They are also grateful for the benefit of an experienced eye studying the suspect spot and a keen ear listening to the rasping cough. A few years ago there was a news item in the papers about a young mother who was waiting at a bus stop with her small son in her arms. He was screaming and she was naturally distressed. Standing next to the mother and child was a grandmother, a complete stranger who, alerted by the child's peculiar high-pitched scream and a curious spot on his torso she'd once seen on somebody in her own family, immediately rang for an ambulance. She had diagnosed meningitis correctly and saved the little boy's life. Now, that's what I call a perfect example of granny instinct.

Katharine Whitehorn Speaks

Katharine Whitehorn, columnist and Agony Aunt for *Saga* magazine, is married to the novelist Gavin Lyall. They have two sons and two grandchildren.

Not all houses have the same rules. It's like the host and guest thing. Different houses, different habits and you must respect your children's rules and establish yours on your territory.

For instance, when my sons went to stay with their grandparents they had a great time, but it was a rule that my parents had a rest every afternoon and they accepted that after lunch they'd spend time in their bedroom and keep quiet.

Our children won't allow smoking in the house but they've got a conservatory full of old bicycles and dead plants and stuff and Gavin is allowed to smoke in there. They've told him they don't want him smoking near the baby, either, when they're in our house, so Gavin smokes in his study with the door closed.

You don't say anything unless you're asked. If you are asked for advice use lots of tact. Safety is the only exception. If the grandchildren aren't using a life jacket on your boat you're justified in insisting that they should.

Having said that, if you *are* asked, grandmothers do know a lot that mothers don't know and you can say with confidence, 'This stage, too, will pass.'

" THE TORTELLINI PLEASE,
AND SOME ITALIANS
FOR THE CHILD.... "

6

Food

When the Royals come to stay they send you a shopping list of what they like to eat and what they don't ... or won't. Sounds familiar, doesn't it? The Prince of Wales, I read, is partial to soft-boiled eggs, wild mushrooms, fish, game, pasta, ice cream, soft cheese, French cheese, double cream, full fat milk, Earl Grey tea, Laphroaig whisky and dry martinis (but only if they are mixed three parts gin to one párt martini). He dislikes large portions, overcooked veg, coffee, chocolate, nuts, garlic, curry, chillies, raw onions, pork, offal, tropical fruit, oysters and blue cheese. Princess Margaret won't touch salmon and game, most meat and puddings. The Queen Mother doesn't care for after-dinner coffee; Princess Anne and the Queen loathe shellfish.

Guests from hell, some might say. To others, who have had a recent visit from their children and grand-children, these royal food fads will seem eminently reasonable. 'Now don't forget, mum, Stephen can't eat red meat and he doesn't like carrots. Jane's preg-nant again and she won't touch eggs. Lucy's vegetarian – all the girls in her class are veggies this term . . .'

Modern parents are not only fussy about what *they* eat (they are vegans or they can't touch gluten), they are positively paranoid about the poisons they believe you are about to slip their children. 'Not *chocolate* cake?' they say, roaming your kitchen like a food inspector. 'We'll never get him to sleep after that.' Not treacle tart, either, it seems: 'You do realise that just one slice of that tart could give him a sweet habit for life?' They are wary of sausages: 'Stuffed with harmful additives . . .' and have just read a newspaper article about low levels of cancerous, gender-bender chemicals lurking in the fish finger.

How much easier to prepare Prince Philip's favour-ite breakfast, fillets of sole in cream, than to confront a family, first thing in the morning, that doesn't eat toast or cereal because of the wheat content ('Where do you keep the rice cakes, mum?') and never drinks tea or coffee ('Oh mum, don't say you haven't got any camomile?') or milk ('You know Jim's not allowed dairy products').

Try celebrating Easter with this lot of picky eaters. The Easter Bunny hides wholesome dried fruits concealed in a cardboard egg and the adults have to hand each other sinful chocolate ones behind their backs so the grandchild can't glimpse what he's missing. And when he screams as he is put into the car to go home, as toddlers always do, his father says: 'Ah, it's that miniature chocolate egg you gave him. No wonder he's overexcited.'

It won't surprise all the grandmothers who have had to cope with this sort of scenario to learn that 15 per cent of children admitted to hospital show signs of malnutrition, and that Hazel Rollins, a specialist nutrition nurse in Bedfordshire, puts this down to well-meaning but misguided diets. 'You see some pretty cranky practices going on with food allergy,' she says. 'Parents put children on exclusion diets, where they avoid things like all dairy products and tomatoes and mushrooms, on the basis of some strange test an amateur therapist has carried out on their fingernails.'

And Dr Adrian Thomas, who works at a children's hospital in Manchester, says that children who are denied sensible diets by over-fussy parents face an increased risk of serious illness. He blames what he calls 'the muesli-belt syndrome' where low-fat, low-calorie diets, including skimmed milk, are given to children. 'A malnourished child can start off with a chest infection – and very quickly end up in a downward spiral,' he says. 'Because they are ill they lose their appetite even more, and as they become even more malnourished they are at a greater risk of more serious infection.'

So that's something else for parents to worry about, along with all the doom-laden warnings about honey and botulism, eggs and salmonella, soft cheese and listeria, and 'I do hope you haven't wrapped those sandwiches in *cling film*'.

Only a few weeks ago there was a half-page photo in my daily paper of a lettuce looking the picture of health. Next to it was a shock-horror list of the high chemical levels of pesticide nestling in its leaves. I suppose you could do your family harm if you fed them lettuce like rabbits, and you do wonder if a generation used to buying their salad stuff ready-prepared from the supermarket chiller always washes raw vegetables and fruit as carefully as they should, but what has happened to moderation? 'A little of what you fancy does you good,' my mother used to repeat tiresomely as we sat down to a plate of roast beef, roast potatoes, sprouts and Yorkshire pudding – a dish which is practically a suicide pact to today's young.

In fact, it's a rare family, these days, that sits down together to eat anything. 'Not another meal?' they say reproachfully, as you set the table for a lunchtime omelette and salad – yes, they're eating eggs again, by the way. Yet in their own home they never stop eating. All through the day various family members graze around the kitchen; into the fridge for a portion of cheese, over to the dresser to finish a dish of leftover nuts, into the cupboard for the Rice Krispies and all the other sugar-laden cereals they wouldn't touch in your house, over to the microwave with the plate of ready-prepared single-portion lasagne, occasionally picking at a herb salad or piece of fresh fruit when they remember how good it's meant to be for them.

The government, as fretful as a grandmother about Nobody Eating Proper Meals Any More, has started sending TV chefs into schools during the holidays to teach children how to cook wholesome suppers. Writing about this experiment in *The Times*, Joe Joseph suggests that filthy food and fractured family life are two sides of the same problem and that a family that gathers around the table to eat lustily also talks lustily and argues lustily and this produces the glue of family life. 'When, in a Woody Allen movie, the family dinner table jangles to an argument over which is the better ocean, the Atlantic or the Pacific, Jews walk out of the cinema saying not, "what craziness that Woody Allen gets up to", but, "can you believe anyone would really think the Pacific was a better ocean than the Atlantic?" '

It's Joe's view that it might be wiser to start by prohibiting food manufacturers and fast-food restaurants from producing items 'that you would be reluctant to step in, let alone put in your mouth. Selling frozen baked-bean pizzas is the equivalent of hawking mild stimulants to schoolkids. Once they get the taste for it they'll soon be on to the hard stuff . . . chicken-style nuggets, made from tasty chicken slurry hosed down from abattoir walls and re-formed into shapes not otherwise seen anywhere in nature.'

Who buys this stuff? And having bought it, why are they so astonished to discover that junk food is bad for them? Experienced shoppers are constantly surprised by consumer articles and programmes complaining that food aimed at children is dressed up with misleading or bogus health claims to fool parents. Is there a granny in the land who would not know instinctively that sweets called Jelly Tots will be stuffed with sugar, even if they are promoted as containing 'real fruit juice and added vitamin C'? What granny would consider seriously that Yum Tums Iced Gem Biscuits would make a nutritious snack, even if the manufacturers do claim they contain 'added vitamins and minerals'? Any grandmother knows these foods aren't going to be good for children, just as any grandmother knows that two tiny Yum Tum Iced Gems are not going to clog their grandchildren's little arteries or give them a lifelong craving for sweets.

If parents are that easily fooled, perhaps we need a panel of shrewd grannies to vet child-appeal products before they get on the supermarket shelves. This excellent idea comes from Terry Durack complaining, in the *Independent on Sunday Review*, about dodgy recipes. He suggested that an élite team of grandmothers should be employed to tick and cross every new crop of cookery recipes before they are printed and readers are obliged to chuck all their expensive ingredients into the waste-bin.

Even with a wise grandmotherly tick next to it, small children will not necessarily eat what is good for them or what they are given. Indeed, most of them are fussier than Prince Charles about what they will or won't eat. Put a fish with a face onto a child's plate and he'll slip down onto his shoulder blades muttering that he doesn't want any part of it. Oddly enough, children will often eat more heartily at granny's house than they do at home. Take a look at these three menus and you will see the reason why.

Menu 1. Fish fingers served with peas, sweetcorn and tomato ketchup. Chocolate ice cream.

Menu 2. Fish cakes, minted new peas, tomato sauce. Chocolate gateau and cream.

Menu 3. Grilled trout served on a bed of wilted pak-choi and baby spinach. Fresh autumn berries with a coulis of kumquat and strawberries.

You'll have spotted the resemblance between menu 1, a traditional children's choice and menu 2, a favourite with the over-forties at the Caprice. Grannies and their grandchildren both like to tuck into simple, familiar dishes, even if grandma's fish dinner has a glint of sophistication about it. Neither of them would have much truck with Menu 3, a meal to appeal to the young, health-conscious adult. 'What's this, then?' they'd both mutter, forking the pak-choi suspiciously and looking around the table for the double cream to ladle over the fruit.

'I fiddle about in the kitchen making all the little meals my children's cookery book recommends and Rosie just prods it with a finger and then turns her face away when I approach her with the spoon,' says one young mother. 'I've tried the "one-for-mummy, one-for-Rosie" routine and all that happens is that I end up eating the puréed chicken and carrots. But when we go to my mother's she mops up the roast lamb and potatoes and still has room for the syrup sponge.'

Syrup sponge is not, of course, served in this young mother's house (all that sugar) and roast potatoes are rarely sighted (all that fat), but grannies are sometimes allowed to give the grandchildren food that is frowned on at home. 'My grandson is fed on sophisticated, wholesome things like hummus and olives,' says novelist Penny Vincenzi, 'and his father believes that Oliver has never met a chocolate biscuit. I've always got a box of them on a shelf in the kitchen and my daughter says, "Well, I expect you *could* have just one of granny's treats – if you're good", and out come the biscuits or the crisps or the sugared buns, the things he likes.'

Another thing children like is pasta. So do their dietary-aware parents, especially if there's a lot of olive oil involved. Spaghetti, served with a home-made tomato and mushroom sauce and scattered with fresh Parmesan, sounds like a safe bet for family meals, doesn't it? Not if your son-in-law is suffering from candida and can't eat cheese or mushrooms, and one of your daughters is allergic to wheat.

Couscous, a healthful alternative to pasta and less messy to spoon up if you're three years old, seems to have all the advantages. It's easy to prepare (steam or boil for ten minutes then leave to absorb the liquid) and can be spliced with favourite vegetables and dried fruit and bits of meat if the vegetarian granddaughter isn't present. Unfortunately couscous also falls down on the wheat content and although the young may be charmed by a certain River Café resonance to this dish, its foreign flavour is likely to alienate your husband, or any other mature male at the table. The word 'couscous' has the same negative effect as offering them a bowl of crème fraîche.

The traditional male eater is equally wary of salads – 'rabbit food' – and does not consider it a bona fide meal unless it is accompanied by thick slices of ham or beef, potatoes and pickle. Vegetarians can't eat chicken, vegans can't eat fish and, as you unwrap the expensive Scottish smoked salmon, your nephew tells you that he was reading an interesting article only the other day about the link between smoked food and cancer.

Everybody can eat brown rice and nobody likes it very much.

Cooking for a children's tea party is effortless after cooking for the family. For a start, there is no need to make a birthday cake in the shape of an engine or a dear little house or a ballet slipper. And don't waste your time icing it elaborately with the child's name and age, either. None of the small party guests will notice how the cake looks so long as it's got lots of candles on it which they can all blow at unhygienically.

A sponge cake is a wiser choice than a fruit cake as you won't be tempted to put nuts in it. You'll have read the horror stories about nut allergies. Check with the parents for odd allergies – better, get your daughter or daughter-in-law to do it. Although it's not actually life-threatening, some children do get quite poorly if they are fed dairy products and if you prepare a bowl of fresh fruit salad, there's sure to be one little girl who comes out in spots if she eats strawberries and another whose face blows up alarmingly if she swallows a segment of citrus fruit.

You can't go wrong with crisps and chocolate biscuits and small sausages, but do not be foolish enough to do as I did and spike the sausages with cocktail sticks for them to plunge into each other's eyes. Small sandwiches (Marmite, jam, banana) go down better than hefty ones or bridge rolls. Ice cream is an all-time favourite, all children go 'yuk' if you put a blancmange in front of them and jelly is more often utilised as a missile than a food, to be hurled from spoon to hair or mashed into the tablecloth.

Finally, if you make frosted cupcakes you'll be eating them up for the next few weeks. All the predatory adults circling the tea table would do well to remember the advice of Professor Yudkin, the wise nutritionist.

'It doesn't matter if children don't finish their food,' he says. 'They'll eat when they are hungry. What really matters, so far as diet is concerned, is that the mother doesn't eat up all the leftovers.'

Prunella Scales Speaks

Actress Prunella Scales is married to the actor Timothy West. She has two sons, two step-grandchildren, aged nineteen and seventeen, and two biological grandsons, Clement and Felix, aged four and two.

'I'm very grateful for step-grandchildren and for having had a surrogate daughter. She lived with us from the age of fifteen and we were very lucky that we had Juliet as godmother to our two boys. I suppose there is a sort of blood thing and I'm not so involved emotionally with my step-grandchildren, but my gut feeling for my own grandchildren is not as strong as it should be.

When my first son was born, the moment he popped out there was an instant, terribly strong switch-on of passion and anxiety and concern. When the grandchildren were born I felt, 'Oh, how lovely. These two people I love very much have a baby', but although I love my grandchildren to death I wasn't involved in the same way.

Because I'm a working grandmother and forced to live an urban life, and my two grandsons live in the country, I don't see them as much as I would like and am not able to be as helpful as I would wish to be.

Actually, they are quite stern with both their grandmothers and seem to bond better with the two grandfathers at the moment. I keep thinking that one day, Clem, when he's a teenager, will come and stay and then I'll begin to bond with him and tell him interesting things which no one else can – because his other granny is French – about England in the sixties, about the war (I remember that), about my life before I was married. I'm a link with the past. One day he'll say, 'It's extraordinary how much grandma knows.'

"...WE'RE SO HOPING HIS
FIRST WORDS WILL BE
POLITICALLY CORRECT...."

7

Discipline

Question: What would you say if

(a) you are having lunch. Your three-year-old grandson
spits out all the food offered to him, climbs down
from his chair and tugs repeatedly at his mother's
skirt. His mother says: 'Why don't you go and
play with your little car, darling?'

(b) you have brought your granddaughter, aged four,
a Peter Rabbit video. The child throws it on the
floor without looking at it. Her mother says:
'Oh, mummy. How sweet of you to bring the

video. I know Rachel's going to love it.'
(c) you are walking in the park with your husband, your daughter and your five-year-old grandson. Your husband is attempting to tell you and your daughter about possible redundancies at his office. The grandson is yanking his mother's hand: 'Mum . . . mum . . . come *on*, mum . . . I want to show you something.' The mother says: 'Sorry, dad, won't be a minute', and turns to the child. 'Now, Peter, what was it you wanted to show me?'

The answer to all three of these all too familiar contemporary vignettes is that you say absolutely nothing.

Conflicting attitudes to discipline divide the generations and cause more family rows than anything else, including who's going to who for Christmas. You just have to remember one golden rule: Grandmothers Should Be Seen and Not Heard. Grandfathers, too, for that matter, but they are less likely to have an opinion on behavioural matters and are certainly less likely to share any thoughts they might have.

The other day a group of us were sitting around the dinner table at a friend's house. Three sets of grandparents, assorted parents and one recalcitrant grandchild, wriggling and whingeing on his mother's knee. The other children had been in bed for several hours. 'Well, Thomas,' the mother said. 'Would you like to go to bed now?'

Six mature heads swivelled towards her in disbelief. Of *course* he wouldn't like to go to bed. What a draft question. Clearly, what Thomas would like most was to stay right there, brothers and sisters and little friends banished above, the sole centre of attention. He took his thumb out of his mouth. 'No, I wouldn't,' he said.

The grandparent group nodded almost impercept- ibly and tried not to catch each other's eye. It was to our credit that we managed to hold back on the advice we all longed to give, which was: 'No, no, Melissa. You've got to be positive and say, "Right, Thomas. Bedtime now . . ." and never mind if he screams loud enough to wake the other children.'

Whenever two or more grandparents get together they shake their heads sadly about the current relaxed attitude to temper tantrums, disobedience, rudeness and bad manners. A small child chucking food around the table and shouting 'shan't . . . won't . . . go away . . . I hate you . . .' suggests to the modern mother only that he needs to be picked up, comforted and diverted: 'Well, what would you like, sweetheart? How about a nice banana?'

'My daughter's generation never say "no",' says a grandmother of two. 'They are so patient, they work around the problem, cajoling, explaining, diverting. It's *such* hard work. "Look, let's see if teddy can put his coat on . . ." – "Shall we see what's on the telly?" – "I wonder where mummy has hidden the chocolate biscuits?" I think diversion tactics are a short-term policy. You're just creating a person who, instead of confronting problems, will endlessly seek out new diversions.

'One day, when my daughter was sobbing with exhaustion, I asked her why she didn't get a playpen. "A playpen?" she said. "You mean put George and Harriet in a *cage*?" I saw a toddler on reins the other day – do you remember them? – and I almost called the NSPCC.'

In her *Spectator* column Leanda de Lisle once remarked that her mother and father were perfect grandparents. Her mother had offered to drive an hour-and-a-half round trip to take her grandsons out from school, when she already had a house full of friends and no help; her father was always buying them thoughtful presents and never complained when they broke his porcelain. 'But sometimes,' she wrote, 'my father expresses his surprise at how adults are now expected to put themselves out to fit into a child's world rather than the other way round.'

'I'm constantly amazed at the way the household revolves around my three-year-old grandson,' a grandmother told me. 'Does he want to get up? Would he like to go for a walk? When they come here for lunch, it's would Simon like this or prefer that? Has he finished? Would he like to get down? There are four grown-up people sitting around the table paying homage to this small male person. And when it's time to go home they say, "Are you tired, darling? Would you like to go home now or shall we wait until after the *Teletubbies*?" '

If a mother's place is in the wrong, a grandmother's place is doubly so. Read through the books and articles about grandparenting and you'll find that granny comes over as the wicked witch, constantly sapping the young mother's confidence with dangerous old-fashioned notions, and implied criticism: 'Oh, you bath her like *that*, do you?' One such book, published in 1997 for heaven's sake, notes that grandmothers are often authoritarian in their discipline, favouring physical punishment and the withdrawal of love. The author writes of 'women who believe that babies wet their nappies to get attention'.

Who are these women? I think they died with my grandmother in 1940-something. Today's grandparents are not from the 'spare-the-rod-and-spoil-the-child' era of parenting; most of us brought up our own children in the permissive sixties and seventies and, like Anna Haycraft, the fiercest piece of advice we might offer is, 'I don't think it's a frightfully good idea to be indulgent with children because it just makes other people dislike them.'

What we do know, after years of anticipating stubborn expressions or wilful foot-stamping, is that you don't hang about having a family discussion about whether or not you're going to leave now or after the *Teletubbies* – we'd have the child buttoned into his coat, out of the door and strapped into the car seat before he had time to make his views known. We have also discovered, over the years, the value of the easily understood word, 'No'.

So, when small children, who have never heard this useful word, come to call, how do you stop them from wrecking your house, without shouting, 'Stop that immediately!' and alienating their parents for ever? The trick is to alert the parents to the dangers they expect to find lurking around every corner of your house, anyway, and Leanda de Lisle's father might still have his Meissen intact if he'd confided in Leanda his anxiety that some of the pieces had seriously jagged edges and could inflict a nasty cut.

Let's return to the dancing granddaughter scenario I mentioned earlier. The granddaughter is jumping up and down on your polished coffee table in her brand new grown-up shoes and her parents are beaming approvingly: 'Look, grandma, she's dancing for you.'

What do you do? The quickest way to remove a toddler from a polished table top or any other cherished surface is to smile fondly and then clap your hand to your mouth, murmuring, 'Oh, I do hope that leg has been fixed properly.'

This is a useful tactic for any number of everyday situations. The children are jumping up and down on the bed, hurling pillows and leaving muddy footprints on the bedspread. 'I don't *think* that's the bed with the spiky broken springs . . .'

Your grandson is fooling around on the sofa in a way that could damage both the springs and the cushions. 'Look what fun he's having . . . I was read-ing the other day about the residual toxic fumes that hang around after dry cleaning . . . well, it must be at least a week since I had the Servicemaster people in.'

The grandchildren are joyfully digging up your

precious agapanthus. 'I do hate the idea of pesticides, don't you, but I had to give them a spray yesterday...'

'It's OK when you've got a direct line to the kids,' says one grandmother, 'but you have to keep quiet when the parents are there. Jack and Joanne used to climb in through the ground floor bedroom window, leap onto the bed, race out of the door and crash back through the window and onto the bed again ... and again and again. My son and daughter-in-law were totally relaxed about this until I mentioned that the glass in one of the windows was loose – totally true, as it happens. The children were called in immediately and told to sit down quietly.'

This grandmother was less successful with her television ploy. 'They always get up early to watch the breakfast programmes. Everyone's screaming ... the characters on the telly and the children watching it. I tried taking the aerial out of the back before I went to bed, but of course they checked that out instantly and we were woken up at 7.30 as usual.'

As we all know, guilt is born with the baby and the working mother feels guiltiest of all, compensating for her absence by keeping the children up until all hours and proffering presents if she's out of the house for more than eight hours. 'At one point my grandson would say, as his mother walked through the door, "What have you got for me?" ' says a friend who was a working mother and is now a working grandmother. 'I remember doing the same myself.'

'My daughter-in-law has a high-powered job and

she admits she compensates like mad,' says another grandmother. 'But I think her children are well balanced *because* she's working; she's incredibly laid back and happy. The other daughter-in-law has given up work and spends all her time mollycoddling her two. Before they go out it's, "Oh, are their feet warm enough? Are their hands warm? Are they wearing the right hats? Hold on, we'd better put their coats on." And she won't let them run out into the garden and play in case they get a chill. She's turned childminding into a 24-hours-a-day full-time job.'

Grandmothers, used to running the show, find it hard to give up control and have to grit their teeth to stop themselves saying, as this grandmother yearned to do, 'Oh, for goodness sake, it'll do them good to run around, a bit of fresh air never hurt anyone . . .' and they all agree that it's easier to deal with the grandchildren when their parents aren't there.

Kathy Jager, who looks after her grandchildren at least once a week, says: 'There's a fine line between interfering and caring. You do have to tell them if they're behaving like monsters that you're not going to allow it. I find it helps to let them know why you don't like what they are doing. I say, "I love you but I don't love what you're doing right now and that's why grandma is telling you to stop." '

'Because my daughter is working I often have Jonathan, my grandchild, to stay,' says another grandmother, 'and I always make him sit down to eat his dinner. He invariably counters with: "But mummy always lets me walk about when I'm eating." "What mummy lets you do in her house is her affair," I say briskly. "When you're in my house you do what I say." '

Jonathan is, of course, perfectly happy to sit down in granny's house – except when his mother is there, too. Then he plays mummy off against granny, just as he plays mummy off against daddy. It's wise not to get involved in the good cop/bad cop routine – 'I would let you have the chocolate biscuit/stay up late/buy that toy gun, only mummy wouldn't like it.'

In disciplinary matters it is often less contentious, and therefore easier, to opt for the scapegoat role. 'I don't think granny would like you poking her doggy's eyes with that stick . . .' or 'I think grandpa would rather you didn't wander around the room with that mug of Ribena . . .' is a mild irritation compared to having a blind dog and a ruined carpet.

Not that granny is necessarily the disciplinarian in the family. Often the reverse is true and parents despair of the mayhem created by grandparents arriving with parcels of presents and unsuitable sweets which the parents firmly believe will rot tiny teeth and make their children sick. Before they could be intercepted by their son and daughter-in-law, one set of grand-parents actually went upstairs and woke up the grandchildren to give them each a bag of sweets.

'My husband says I am my grandchildren's slave,' a friend says. 'They say, "Come and do some drawings for us," and I do. Of course, I never did this with my own children. My daughter-in-law chats away to me and I think, how could she not stop and listen to their dear little voices.' She adds, with commendable honesty, 'The best thing is a couple of idyllic hours and then back they go to mummy and daddy.'

'They take it all so much more seriously than we did,' says another friend. 'They know so much more. My daughter even knows the composition of breast milk. They read so many books. There's a library piled up on the shelf by my daughter's bed, *How to Get Your Baby to Sleep*, *How to Tame Your Toddler*, with *How to Stop Baby Crying* on the top, while the baby howls next door.

'I used to read Dr Spock, "You've dropped the baby on his head? Don't worry, babies are tough little things." Of course I don't tell her that. I don't say anything.'

Shirley Conran Speaks

Shirley Conran, the writer and Chair of MIM (Mothers in Management) has two sons with her ex-husband, Sir Terence, and two grandchildren, Sam (eleven) and Max (four). Their parents are Sebastian Conran, the designer, and his wife Georgina Godley, who is also a designer.

You don't plan to be a grandmother, do you? Like, 'Next week I'll be a grandmother.' I'm a failure at it and I shouldn't be, I had such wonderful examples. When war started my grandmother bought a house in Hereford where she thought Hitler wouldn't strike, and all five grandchildren went to live with her. She had no help, she was sixty-five and would only let my parents pay her 25 shillings, the standard evacuee allowance. She was a Pied Piper of a storyteller and we all adored her. My mother, too, was a born nanny, which means she was also a brilliant grand-nanny. I was quite good at being a mother. Eccentric and odd I might have been, but my mother and grand- mother had given me confidence. I learned foot- ball, how to ride a motor bike and because I trained as a sculptor I could tap a lump of frozen spinach and break it into two in one go. That impressed them. It's easy to be interested in one's children, not so easy to be interested in one's grandchildren.

I came back to England because I wanted to be with the grandchildren, and I hardly ever see them. Their schedules are packed as tightly as suitcases, with karate lessons, Japanese lessons, football on Saturday. It's such a different life – pederasts and pushers and maniacs at the school gates. No cooking. No breakfast. The facts of life have changed and we haven't got into it yet. What do they expect of us? What do we expect of them? I know what gran wants. Gran wants what she shouldn't expect and won't get, which is cuddles and kisses. They do loathe that. Quite right, too. Grandchildren are not puppies and kittens.

Sebastian brings Sam or Max over sometimes on a Sunday morning (buying himself a Big Mac on the way because I once burned his bacon and egg and he doesn't trust me to do a decent cooked breakfast), and I'm so excited, waiting to see the happy little faces, the cries of 'Oh, granny, granny, granny . . .' Do I get it? I do not. Sam looks at me warily, Max ignores me happily, they are extremely polite, always with one eye on the video or the television.

A friend of mine said, 'Wait until Sam's eight, he'll want to go on trips.' He's ten and he doesn't want to go on trips. 'Want to go to Paris, Sam?' 'No, thanks.'

Georgina, my daughter-in-law, once suggested us all going to a tropical area in the New Forest under a giant plastic dome. Well, I knew I'd hate it and said: 'Let's go to Fiji instead.' But they've got their own friends, their own work, they are all far too busy.

I'd drop most things to baby-sit, I'm often available. Trouble is, I can't stay awake after 10 p.m.

"...SHE CRIES, EATS, AND HAS
REAL ALLERGIES..."

8
New Technology

Let's see how you would cope with this apparently
simple exercise.

You have precisely ten minutes left before running
over into the next two hours in the underground car
park. Can you, in that time, transfer a lively two-year-
old from a three-wheeled Swedish canvas pushchair
into the latest high-tech children's car seat, strap and
clip him or her in correctly and then dismantle the
pushchair and fold it into the boot?

Of course you can't. Not if you are over forty. You'll

have passed the £4 charge and be well into the £6.50 overtime before you've mastered all that complicated machinery and got the little one stowed away safely in the back of your car. A friend of mine, shrewd enough to count her annual pay cheque in hundreds of thousands, found herself in this situation and confessed that eventually she became so distraught that she had to seek out a young mother and beg tearfully for assistance.

The young mother's demonstration was clear and concise. Her instructions, carried out faithfully by my friend, proved more complex.

The exercise went as follows: Unclip pram straps. Hit head while lifting squirming toddler out of pram and forcing him or her into child's seat in the back of the car. Locate straps from under toddler and beneath child seat. Demobilise toddler by clipping straps (1) and (2) around tummy. Pull strap (3) through legs of toddler, now wriggling and screaming, and attach to clip containing straps (1) and (2). Unclip strap (3) to release toddler's right leg which is incorrectly placed next to left leg. Prising legs apart and keeping firmly in position with left hand, replace strap (3) between legs of toddler with right hand and re-attach to clips (1) and (2). Back out of car. Hit head. Grip front of pram with left hand, while jerking up seat with right hand and at the same time kicking back wheels with right foot. Attempt to collapse pram. Check why pram appears not to be folded. Discover this is as folded as it gets. Carry semi-collapsed pram around to the back of the car. Open boot. Attempt unsuccessfully to fit pram into boot. Close boot. Carry pram back to the front passenger door. Open it. Throw in pram. Shout at toddler.

This intractable Scandinavian pushchair is, according to my friend, as impractical on the London streets as a Range Rover, only not so comfortable for the passenger. A classic bone-shaker, it trundles along at exhaust level, so that the child can breathe in fumes at the same time as jarring his or her back. My friend thinks it works at its best when stationary because her grandchild finds the curious slant of the backrest more soporific than his cot. There is also available in all the best baby departments an impressively large double pram with the unlikely name, Mountain Terrain. One young mother said she had to take the children out of it and decompress one side to get into the shopping precinct. She said she had no future plans to push it up the north face of the Eiger.

Why are all these bits of equipment so cumbersome and complicated? It took two parents and two grandparents (one of them me) to crack the code in the assembly instruction leaflet and erect the almost unput-uppable Cumfi Travel Cot. This is a huge square thing, halfway between a cot and a playpen involving flanges and pegs, and we had to rearrange the furniture to accommodate it.

As for the modern car seats, they are so heavily padded, and are mounted on so many bruising metal tubes and springs, that they weigh as much as the average armchair. Attached to them are tags with words on them like WARNING and DANGER and BE SURE TO READ THIS. What you read are paragraphs like, 'In many cases the position of the car seat belts makes it impossible to fit some seats securely. In other cars the seat does not fit because, although the seat fits solidly, the seat-belt buckle lies on the frame of the seat. This strains the buckle which could break in an accident.' Horrific.

The best retailers offer a sort of Kwik Fit service so that you can be sure you've got the right seat for your particular make of car. This means, of course, that the seat that fits safely in the daughter's Volvo is not necessarily right for your Rover. Easier to buy your own seat, really, which is perhaps what the manufacturers had in mind.

It's all so unnecessarily obscure and worrying that I wasn't surprised to come across a very pregnant girl, who'd been working her way through a list of apparently lethal pieces of equipment, gazing in wild-eyed anxiety at an assistant in the baby shop who had just told her that it was important to buy a mattress two inches smaller than the one she had chosen to fit her cot.

'Why?' she said. 'Is it dangerous if it fits?'

'Of course not,' the assistant said. 'A smaller mattress is easier to tuck in.'

A friend who has four grandchildren says that when they come to stay it looks as though their parents are moving house. 'The whole of my kitchen worktop is taken over by equipment,' she says. 'Then there's a microwave for instant hot milk, a spare telly, lots of babies' bottles, little seats for sitting on the loo, plastic baby-supports to stick in the bath, a baby-monitor to plug in so we can hear if the baby stops breathing, little cars to run around the garden and over the carpets, mugs with non-drip spouts which are not non-drip if the child carries it around upside down, as well as a whole mass of stuff I've never seen before and don't understand.'

This suggests an amusing and instructive quiz to tax your friends' knowledge on winter evenings when they have become tiresomely over-familiar with all the answers to the Trivial Pursuit questions. It's called Identify these Objects?

 1.

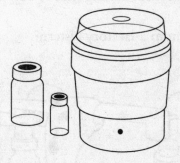

Is this:

(a) an electric food mixer with all the relevant attachments?

(b) a steam steriliser with appropriate compartments for sterilising bottles and dummies and heating up milk?

(c) a juice extractor for making your own apple juice?

2.

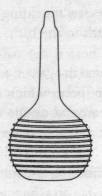

Is this:

(a) a suction pump for scooping the fat off the top of soup?

(b) an aspirator for suctioning mucus out of the baby's nose?

(c) a ballcock from a lavatory cistern?

3.

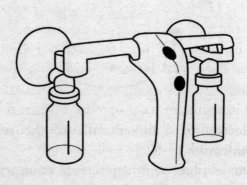

Is this:

(a) part of a homebrew beer kit?
(b) an electronic breast pump?
(c) a home water purifier?

The correct answer in each set of questions is (b). The reason these items of baby equipment may seem unfamiliar is that nobody would be foolish enough to buy them except for a nervous young mother shopping for her first baby. My step-daughter was one such mother. She says: 'The electronic steam steriliser has a picture on the box of a happy woman looking nothing like me trying to work it out. The first time I used it I didn't put in the right amount of water and melted all the plastic goods. I still don't know how to use it properly. It's become a dumping area for small plastic bits.'

She is not delighted with the electronic breast pump, either, which looks as though it would nip off a nipple if you didn't watch out. 'You fix it to your breast and it pumps off milk which you can put in the fridge, label and use as needed. Ideal for Working Woman or New Man when he does the night feed. If you must use a breast pump the manual one is less alarming.

'I tried inserting the nasal aspirator as instructed and the baby screamed as though I'd stuck pins in her. Cotton buds work perfectly well.'

In my step-daughter's garden there is an unwelcome gift called a Portable Bouncer. She looked at it with distaste. 'It's just a swing in a frame. You push a button and it swings, instead of you pushing your child with an "Up you go!", thus eradicating all human intervention and fun.

'It's all evolution going in the wrong direction and unnecessarily traumatic, isn't it? When I first had my baby I was just so scared of doing anything because I couldn't cope with the kit.'

If it's traumatic for a young mother, it is doubly so for a novice grandmother or step-grandmother. Everything is different, even the disposable nappies. I'll admit that the Velcro fastenings on the Pampers are easier to manage than the old-fashioned poppers on the Paddi Pads which had a habit of unpopping, but it is disquieting to discover that modern disposables come in different sizes like proper clothes, a dilemma when you're left holding the granddaughter and don't know her correct weight.

'I've never been very good with Velcro,' a friend says, 'and when I eventually got the flaming nappy onto the baby it went right up to her armpits.'

I seem to remember our generation travelling light with baby, a carry-cot, a packet of Paddi-Pads, a bottle which we stuck in a saucepan of boiling water to sterilise it and a carrier bag of etceteras. And yet, I also remember my mother standing at her front door crying: 'My God, where on earth are we going to put all that stuff?'

Mary Francis Speaks

Mary Francis is married to the author Dick Francis. They have two sons, five grandchildren and three step-grandchildren aged from thirteen to twenty-five.

We like both our sons' families to know each other. Every year we go and stay in a family hotel in Devon and everyone comes, between eighteen and twenty-one of us. I do sometimes feel like a ringmaster but they're all good-natured. Maybe one year one of them will be slightly scratchy with another and the next year they're the best of friends.

It's very odd to find one's sons middle-aged. You know you can't change what you have put in, and you can't change the grandchildren, either. They just need encouragement to make them feel valuable people. You listen to them, remember what they said, talk to them, explain things and wait for them to understand.

It is fun when they are babies but as they grow older it's a whole new dimension. Their thoughts, their feelings, give you a fantastic view of the future and what their lives will be.

Two of them have exceptional talents – one of the granddaughters has sung four solos in St Mark's Cathedral in Venice, and one of the grandsons is going to be an inventor – and you get impatient to see it come out. I feel I'd like another fifty years to see what happens to them all.

I have friends who have no grandchildren and I have to be careful not to show that I feel sorry for them.

..." GRAN'S KNITTING ME A
TERRORIST BALACLAVA "...

9

Giving Things

What's needed in toy shops and toy departments is the
sort of wise store-consultant who emerges from cubby-
holes behind Bedding to tell you exactly what you
ought to wear for your boss's daughter's wedding, or
how, by mixing last year's blue denim with a few
cleverly chosen leopard-print accessories, you can
achieve *Vogue*'s look for spring. It's *that* difficult buying
presents for the grandchildren.

Somebody to tell you . . .

(1) that anything bought for a child under three will be glanced at and tossed casually on the floor unless the baby/toddler can eat it, which young parents probably won't allow, anyway. Anything bought for a child under three is, therefore, a present for mummy and daddy and you will elicit adult screams of delight if you flatter them by buying the 18-month-old grandchild a boring looking educational toy *clearly labelled* 'Ages 2–4' on the box.

(2) to tread delicately through the minefield of multiple gifts for a cluster of grandchildren. Are you absolutely certain that Sophie's prettily wrapped Teletubby Cloth Bricks and Mandy's small reindeer in a Father Christmas hat equal Mark's wooden tricycle? The answer is that they don't: the recipients will know it ('She loves Mark £12.54 more than me . . .'), and in no time at all the girls will have commandeered Mark's bike and he will have vengefully torn off the reindeer's head and been sent to bed.

(3) not to allow yourself to get carried away on foreign holidays by all those adorable miniature French/Italian/Spanish shoes or jazzy little American party dresses. They look so enchanting in the shops and so silly when you get home to find your grandchildren have inexplicably grown into Clark's sandals and their first school uniform.

(4)   never to buy pets as presents. A friend of mine was pestered by her grandson to buy him a pair of rats for his eighth birthday. Her daughter and son-in-law, kept busy cleaning out cages and dodging sharp nips at feeding time, were resentfully tight-lipped for months, and guess who was left looking after the rats (which had seemingly been multiplying monthly) when the family went off skiing? Grandmother, of course.

(5)   to check out videotapes or (if your grandchildren have access to the very latest computers and you can get your hands on one, too) DVDs before gift-wrapping. Older children might well be delighted with *Summer Holiday*, but their parents will be less pleased if, instead of a rerun of Cliff and his Shadows larking about wholesomely on their hols, it turns out to be a pastiche, a seedy summer sex romp under the same title.

(6)   not to go in for the kind of annual money gifts that bypass the grandchildren and go straight into the bank, accruing in such a way that the grandchildren are near millionaires by the time they are twenty-one. This is an unsatisfactory present for both givers and receivers. Children are rarely excited by something that is going to be good for them some time in the future. And all that money may be resented by the breadwinner of the family: 'Do your parents imagine I can't afford to look after my own children?'

(7) to look inside every lavishly illustrated boxed gift before handing it over. You may well discover that (a) the battery-operated toy does not contain a battery, (b) you do not understand how all those pieces of unpainted wood can be assembled to make a fire engine, (c) the impressively large board game, that takes two sheets of wrapping paper to cover it, contains only a piece of printed cardboard and a couple of dice and (d) whatever is inside the box, there's a piece missing.

(8) the wisdom of arriving very early or very late on gift-giving occasions. With mummy and daddy too flustered and busy with door-opening, greetings and overreacting every time their child opens a parcel – 'Darling! A jigsaw! Aren't you a lucky girl? And have you said thank you to Auntie Jane . . . ?' – many a gift has disappeared under mounds of coloured paper before anyone has noted down who gave Emma the dear little gold watch.

(9) not to attempt the latest fashionable fad. By the time you and I are tuned in to Beanies or Pokemon cards or Cyber Pets or whatever, the young will have moved on to another must-have the *Daily Mail* hasn't told us about yet.

(10) socks and scarves and gloves are not presents.

It will astonish many grandparents to learn that in a recent survey about the grandparent/grandchildren relationship the majority of the children questioned thought that their grandparents' main role was to look after them and love them and – here comes the bit that will throw you – only 10 per cent thought their grandparents' main function was to 'give things'.

I suspect a nudge from mummy during the filling in of this section of the questionnaire. In spite of the fact that grandmothers are always moaning about the amount of toys children have these days – 'she can hardly get into bed for the piles of brightly coloured plastic' – they invariably arrive with a gift, and a grandchild would be deeply disappointed if granny reached into her bag only to bring out a packet of Marlboroughs. I know that I was nearly fifty before I stopped turning my grandmother's Christmas cards upside down and shaking them in the hope that she'd remembered to put in the fiver.

So, what *do* they like? I canvassed a few good toy shops:

0–3:   Soft things they can carry around and suck, like a colourful felt Noah's Ark with an appealing pair of small fabric animals behind each 'window' which can be taken out, sucked and slotted back into place if they haven't disappeared under the sofa.

10–18 months: A baby walker to load and unload, or any sturdy push-and-pull toy that can be propelled sharply into adult legs.

10 months–5:   Noisy things they can bang on or blow

into like wooden peg boards, mini xylophones and trumpets. A friend of mine who went into a toy shop last Christmas and asked if they had anything that would annoy a mother and delight a child came out with the perfect gift: a small object which fits into the palm of the hand and emits, when pressed, a noise half-way between a fart and somebody being sick. Her daughter-in-law hasn't forgiven her yet.

3–8: Anything they can jump into and steer into the skirting boards like trucks and cars and bikes.

3–10: Fancy dress outfits like OTT net dresses with wings and wands to match. Cowboy or similar macho gear for the other sex, preferably with a gun attached.

18 months onwards: Books to chew on, books with bits that pull out and things that pop up, large hard-cover highly coloured books, books filled with pictures and fascinating facts, annuals, humorous books based on television programmes, sets of boxed classic books to display on a shelf – even books to read.

Some shops spoke well of all the 'pretend' things, like mock radios and mock mobiles, and for the more mature, the real thing (check out first whether mobiles are still on the cancer scare list before you buy) plus laptops, televisions and computer games.

One shop noted that although children have cup-boards full of teddy bears and dolls and assorted stuffed animals, they usually have only the one favourite they insist on taking to bed with them. This toy shop did not mention that the favourite is very often a scrap of old blanket dignified by the name 'comforter'. But since they're in the business of selling things they wouldn't, would they?

After the toddler stage children usually divide into the active kind who are keen on pedalling and climbing and kicking a ball, the contemplative who like making and building and reading, and the imaginative who paint and make puppet theatres and put on plays. This is no more than a useful guideline, since plenty of imaginative children are seriously allergic to puppet theatres and the performances are a huge yawn for any adult who isn't a doting parent.

For some odd reason, perhaps because we hope to be admired for our taste, originality and insightfulness, grandparents tend to think that putting a cheque in a card in an envelope is not only a cop-out but boring. When was money ever boring? Can you remember, when you were a child, ever thinking, as your grandmother slipped you a fiver, 'Oh, no . . . not another five pounds. *Boring* . . .'?

You can always make the present jollier by, for instance, hiding the cheque inside a mini-guitar if your grandson is saving up for a real one, or inside a doll's outfit if the granddaughter is after more clothes. The joke that never fails is the large box which has to be unwrapped to find a slightly smaller box inside which has to be unwrapped . . . and so on, on the Russian Doll principle, until the child finally gets to the mini-box and the money. I think it needs to be quite a large amount of money to compensate for the disappointment of it not being the large, grand computer/television-type gift the grandchild had anticipated on first sighting the parcel.

Another reason people cite for not giving their grandchildren money is because they are afraid that the children will waste it. We all know that one person's waste of money is another's longed-for treat, and most children would be appalled at the amount of money grandma and grandpa spend on an evening at the opera. Mary and Dick Francis always give their eight grandchildren a Christmas card with a cheque inside it and tell them to buy what they like. Quite right, too. Nobody wants a gift with strings attached ('Get yourself a nice warm winter coat' or 'Put this into a savings account'), and the worst that can happen, if they spend it on something tacky which disintegrates within the week, is that they could grow up into one of those whingeing consumers who are always phoning up Radio Four to complain about something they've just bought which isn't working as it should.

The great thing about giving money is that you can't fall into the trap of aiming the wrong gift at the wrong age group. A glamorous friend of mine once bought her five-year-old grandson a tiny carved wooden train from Liberty and wrapped it in tastefully white-flecked gold paper. A perfect parents' present for the under-threes. A disaster for a literal-minded five-year-old. 'But it isn't proper Christmas paper,' he said. And then he unwrapped the train and his face crumpled. 'And the wheels don't go round.'

Madhur Jaffrey Speaks

Madhur Jaffrey, the Indian actress and cookery writer, sixty-six, is married to Sanford Allen, a classical violinist, and they live in New York. She has three daughters by her first husband, Saeed Jaffrey, and three grandchildren – two boys aged seven and five, and one girl of seventeen months.

My middle daughter did the most generous thing. When she had her first baby, by natural childbirth, she gave us a gift from God. She said we could all be present at the birth – her husband, my husband, myself, her sisters. It was the most heavenly, magical gift.

We all went to the birthing centre in New Jersey. I read poems while she was in labour about the body opening up like a flower, and then we saw the head come out, a glorious, dark-haired boy. It was wonderful. I do have a particular bond with that child because I was there at his birth, but I love all my grandchildren to pieces. When people phone me and I'm busy they assume I'm working, but often I am with my grandchildren. They are my greatest joy and I try to be with them for at least one day a week. And the kids come and see us. We are all very close.

In summer I always rent a large rambling house in Martha's Vineyard and the whole family join us there. I think I'm trying to recreate my own childhood in India. In the summer we would go up to the hills, the whole family. There's a great strength to be had in families and I know I have gained strength from being with my cousins, aunts and grandparents. It was a whole way of life. There were age groups of cousins. My group were all boys and I loved the cricket, the ball games. We had lots of independence and used to roam about by ourselves, little groups of cousins.

I'm hoping that's what my family are getting. We all cook together, shop together, go fishing, we just want to be with each other, just hanging around as a family. They all love it. Well, I think they must do because they come back every year.

"GRANNY CAN BE VERY INTERACTIVE
IF YOU PRESS THE RIGHT BUTTONS..."

10

Outings and Eating

Outings

When I see snow I don't feel like a grown-up. I feel like chucking snowballs, jumping on the nearest toboggan and careering down hillsides. My husband is equally immature and last time it snowed heavily we had to borrow two children from a neighbour because we'd have looked silly tobogganing by ourselves.

Thank goodness for grandchildren. Now I can go and see Father Christmas, dig sandcastles on the beach and drive a bumper car recklessly into all the other bumper cars on the track and everyone will beam admiringly, 'Oh, just look at that wonderful grand-mother', instead of saying, 'Why on earth doesn't that woman act her age?'

During the summer, a small friend of mine spent a day in the country with his older brother and his grandmother. When the children returned home, slightly damp and (in their parents' view) seriously overexcited, they reported breathlessly, 'You'll never guess what grandma did.' What grandma had done was take the children down to a nearby stream where she happened to spot a rope hanging from a tree. 'I used to be really good at rope climbing,' she said, shinning up it and swinging over the stream. She tossed the rope back to the children and urged them to swing over, too. Sensibly, they refused. So grandma, an elegant company chairperson of fifty-four, made two more return trips, piggybacking each child. And then they had to come back again and they all got very wet and had a lovely time. The parents said no, they never would have guessed what grandma did.

The satisfying thing about this outing was that the children and the grandmother enjoyed themselves equally, which is how it should be, instead of each generation sacrificing themselves for the sake of the other. How many grandparents, I wonder, have queued on aching feet for the doubtful pleasure of trudging around some dreary waxwork museum because they thought the children would like it? And how many children have spent an afternoon hitting each other in the back of the car because their parents decided to pander to gran and drive miles and miles to some distant stately home to seek out an obscure *euphorbia polychroma* lurking shyly in formal gardens where No Ball Games Are Allowed?

If you can't find something you both enjoy doing, like a visit to the Small Mammal House at the zoo or jumping up and down in the sea, do make sure there's a pleasing alternative to occupy the one who's likely to get bored and fretful and start playing up.

Fairgrounds, now. Cold or too hot, often wet and muddy, always expensive and agony on the feet. Consider instead a visit to the Trocadero in Shaftesbury Avenue. This houses a vast, vulgar, noisy six floors of video games, traditional fairground entertainments and sideshows, a cinema complex and several splendid virtual reality treats. Rock Circus takes you behind the scenes and into the world of rock and pop, and travellers on the James Bond ride are briefed by 'M' and 'Q' at the start of the journey as though they were Sean or Roger or Pierce. There are also plenty of cafes and bars and restaurants where you can sit and monitor the grandchildren as they simulate fighting Mike Tyson, flying a jet plane over the Rockies, or whatever.

Because the Trocadero is located right on Piccadilly Circus, I found myself gazing speculatively at the fresh-faced children and their apparently kindly looking dads in case I was introducing my small charges into an evil den of rent boys and paedophiles, but on the afternoon we went there it was as wholesome as a village fair and a lot more fun.

Taking your grandchildren to the park can be hard work with all that walking and watching out for rabid dogs and park wardens and piteous cries of, 'Carry me, granny. I'm tired', but choose a park with an adventure playground and the outing becomes a breeze. In Battersea Park there is also a small zoo, a boating lake, playgrounds and something even more desirable than an adventure playground called the One o'Clock Centre. It's open from Monday to Friday from one o'clock until four and it's free. The other day I saw a smart (in every sense) grandmother lolling on a bench close by the Centre, reading *Vogue*, while willing helpers slotted her grandchildren into toy cars, heaved them up slides and organised jolly communal games. There may be a haven like this in a park somewhere near you. Check by phoning your local council and ask for Leisures and Amenities or Play Services.

There are parents and grandparents who boast that their toddlers adore the ballet and like nothing more than a leisurely stroll around the National Gallery hoping to catch a glimpse of the Rokeby *Venus*. I don't believe them, and I write as the embarrassed step-mother of a small boy who once snored competitively from the front row throughout the great Segovia's final concert, and the mother of another small boy who despised any kiddies' entertainment that didn't come to him by way of the television in his sitting room. Both children would have preferred to go to a rock concert than The Little Angel Puppet Theatre and I'm right behind them in the queue on that.

It's my view that cultural events are wasted on anyone under eight because most small children (on the Blue Peter principle) would rather be actively doing than passively looking. The ideal compromise, and you will probably have noted their appearance in your High Street, are the newish studios where you can drop in and paint your own ceramics. Our local Brush & Bisque-it franchise welcomes anyone over six years old to come in and be shown how to paint tiles and egg cups and teapots and jugs and such. It costs a fiver each plus the price of the unpainted item. 'Parents and grandparents will love the special Christmas or Mother's and Father's Day Presents', their brochure states hopefully. Children under ten must be accompanied by an adult, which is no hardship for those of us who are quite content to enjoy a coffee and smile encouragingly while someone else oversees and amuses the grandchildren. I'm told that little girls love it, and that little boys stop loving it when they are around ten years old because that's when they begin to think it's sissy.

Museums are free and usually have rather good cafes and restaurants but I'm reluctant to enter any building with the word 'museum' on it, being instantly transported back to shuffling school crocodiles and rows of dusty statues that aren't *quite* rude enough to be funny. Having said that, the Natural History Museum still scores with its wonderful dinosaurs and the Science

Museum has knocked itself out with handles to pull and buttons to press on the working models and inter-active experiments.

Shirley Eaton has written a useful *Granny's Guide to London**** which includes lots of museums, but I found her advice a bit on the worthy side and suspect that the children I know would find the make-believe spooky thrills and bloodthirsty severed heads at the London Dungeon more amusing and less disturbing than a realistic re-enactment of the Trench Experience at the Imperial War Museum.

Last summer I had a visit from two American teen-agers (one of each sex) who both, when offered the sights and glories of London from the Tower to Tussauds, said firmly that they wanted to go to the football museum. I'd never heard of it but I phoned Tourist Information/Where to Take the Children (a mine of ideas, incidentally) and the first thing to come up was The F. A. Premier League Hall of Fame. The very spot. I sat in the wine bar opposite reading Michael Holroyd's latest until they emerged two hours later, glowing with pleasure and loaded down with expensive souvenirs.

If you want brilliant ideas about how to amuse the grandchildren for a couple of hours or shuffle them off for a weekend or even for the entire school holidays, get hold of *The London Parents' Guide*. It's a magazine stuffed with reliable information and advice about

*Kensington West Productions, £6.99.

places to visit, art, computer and sports centres, summer camps, indoor and outdoor adventure playgrounds, riding schools, swimming pools and outings you'd never even thought about. And as each issue contains a list of past contents, you can send for the one majoring on riding stables or best beaches or whatever you're after.

Amusing granny is easier than keeping the children happy. Just give her a glass of wine, a good novel and a dear little grandchild playing quietly at her side. As we all know, the little grandchild won't be playing quietly for more than a few minutes, so diversions must be found for the young while granny gets on with doing whatever she wants to do.

There are those, and they are usually under thirty-five, who assume that by the time you're a grandparent you'll have given up sex and taken up gardening, and I have noticed recently that many of my friends spend a lot of time talking about plants and extolling the virtues of this garden centre or that. November and December are good months to take the grandchildren with you to almost any garden centre because that is when they transform themselves into tinselly Christmas shops. There is also a good chance of the children running into the trainee from Climbers, Twiners and Wall Shrubs ho-ho-ho-ing around in a red coat and cotton-wool beard.

Out of the festive season, most good garden centres provide playgrounds, some have pet shops or small zoos attached, and Syon Park in Brentford has the lot: a first-class Wyevale garden centre, plus a pet centre, an aquarium, a butterfly house and a giant indoor adventure playground for children up to twelve years old, with a special area for the two-to-five-year-olds. There are also cafes and shops and peacocks strolling about in a proprietorial sort of way.

Now that retailers have read the recent research paper telling them what we all could have told them anyway – 40 per cent of shopping trips end because of family arguments; 65 per cent of parents prefer to go shopping without their children – they are competing to make shopping a fun time for the little ones so that their parents, or grandparents, can spend, spend, spend, unencumbered by the petulant tug or complaining whine.

The big new Marks and Spencer in Manchester, for instance, has a play station with computerised and virtual reality games, a coffee bar and a customer lounge with comfy sofas and a television showing continuous Sky sport where you can park your partner, the man who causes at least 35 per cent of those family arguments by saying, 'Right – are we ready to go home now, then?' when you haven't even bought a pair of tights yet.

Most large out-of-town stores have installed a playground or two and the usual virtual reality games. Ikea offers a supervised indoor crèche with all the jumping, climbing, sliding, crayoning and painting things and they will look after three-to-six-year-olds for forty-five minutes without charge. This doesn't give you time to reconnoitre the store and then get lost trying to find the exit, but does allow time for a hassle-free queue at the checkout or a peaceful Swedish meatball in the cafeteria.

As shopping becomes more and more the national pastime, it has started calling itself an Experience. What turns the same boring old shops in the same sanitised malls into an Experience are all the etceteras. Cafes and bars and restaurants and cinema complexes; comfortable lounges with and without television for the non-shoppers and the foot-weary; exotic trees growing inside and outside; free parking for thousands of cars; and playgrounds and crèches where you can leave the children to play in safety while you shop.

I was seriously impressed by the Bluewater Shopping Experience. It contains all the items above and is the largest shopping centre in Europe, with fifty acres of landscaped parkland, seven lakes (one with boats on it), five kilometres of cycle paths, outdoor and indoor adventure playgrounds and an ice rink.

Bluewater discovered that the average child gets bored after forty minutes of traipsing round the shops and so they provide frequent distractions – all the chips-with-chips style cafes, Disney cartoons and films along with the pizzas, toy stores where prospective customers can play with the merchandise and computer stores offering free access to the internet. There's a winding basement grotto underneath and in full view of a large restaurant, so that children can muck about and the adults can keep an eye on them while they are eating, and plenty of clowns and stiltwalkers and people giving away balloons and painting faces.

The crèche, supervised by trained staff, has an hourly charge which would add up to £9 for three and a half hours, including drinks and biscuits. They have a pager system so they can recall a parent whose child is distressed or disruptive (so far they've only had to do this once, during the pre-Christmas excitement) and a unique safe-and-found system using digital cameras to locate those children who manage to give their parents the slip.

I had to be dragged out of Girl Heaven (one of the fifty children's shops) which features fairy outfits, sparkly hairbands and everything pink and glitzy and girlie, by the granny who accompanied me. She lives in Wiltshire and said that if she was ever foolish enough to undertake a car drive across the country with her grandchildren she'd head for Legoland rather than Bluewater. I protested that Legoland was more of a children's outing than a granny trip, but my friend, looking only slightly embarrassed, said she had thoroughly enjoyed the rollercoaster ride, when she had flown through the treetops past animated Lego models, and she'd got some wonderful photographs she'd show me of Jeanie, her youngest granddaughter, performing with real actors in the circus area.

A traditional toy shop that isn't confusingly over-crowded and has a comfortable restaurant is another fine compromise for adults and children. Daisy & Tom, in Chelsea, has a Soda Bar which serves sophisticated grown-up snacks as well as Marmite soldiers and peanut-butter sandwiches; it also displays shelves full of nostalgically familiar teddy bears and dolls and provides old-fashioned children's hair-cutting and specialist shoe-fitting services. Of course they've got all the modern electronic stuff, too, but older adults will be much cheered by a whole floor full of excellent children's books. You could have a deeply satisfying browse and get away for only £2.99 per child, which is the cost of the jolly, coloured picnic boxes containing a sandwich, a Wagon Wheel, an apple and a carton of Ribena.

When lunching with a toddler or two, there is no fear of being turned away at the door or embarrassed by their uninhibited behaviour, if you opt for the food-and-fun places that go all out to please with crayons and face painting and entertainers. India Knight once wrote in the *Sunday Times Magazine* about taking her children into a teashop close by a beach in East Sussex and being turned away by the snooty proprietress who said that she didn't allow children on her premises. 'We were in a teashop at tea time,' India wrote, 'as opposed to, say, a triple-Michelin-starred restaurant at midnight.'

Addresses

Trocadero, Shaftesbury Avenue/Piccadilly Circus, London W1 (0891 881100).

The Science Museum, Exhibition Road, London SW7 (020 7938 8008).

The Natural History Museum, Cromwell Road, London SW7 (020 7942 5000).

The London Dungeon, 28 Tooley Street, London SE1 (0891 6000 666).

The London Parents' Guide, 1 Stockwell Terrace, London SW9 0QD (020 7793 1990). £2.50 inc. postage.

Tourist Information/Where to take the children (0891 505 460).

F.A. Premier League Hall of Fame, County Hall, Riverside Building, Westminster Bridge Road, London SE1 (0870 848 8484).

Syon House, Syon Park, Brentford, Middx (020 8560 0883).

Bluewater, Greenhithe, Kent (08436 021 021).

Legoland, Windsor Park, Winkfield Road, Windsor, Berks (0870 504 0404).

Daisy & Tom, 181 Kings Road, Chelsea, London SW3 (020 7352 5000).

Eating

Outings nearly always involve a meal or two, so is there anywhere we should take the grandchildren that isn't called McDonalds? What gourmet experience are they after and which restaurants do they favour? Nobody is more qualified to answer this question than the author and columnist Craig Brown. He was a food critic for ten years, writing a weekly column for *The Times* and then for the *Daily Telegraph*. And he is the father of eleven-year-old Tallulah and Silas, who is nine. This is what Craig has to say about eating out with children:

You know that parental thing boasting about how children will eat anything? Well, ours don't. You can just about palm them off with a pizza. Basically they like fish and chips and chips and chicken nuggets. It's embarrassing, really. And pasta things, which is good because most Italian restaurants love having children around, although I doubt if The River Café would be so delighted.

The Chinese also have a tradition of children eating with grown-ups and although they are a bit dodgy on the food side there's always something with batter around it which children like. There's a new chain called Wok-Wok, kind of noodle-y with prawns and squid and curries and fishcakes and satays and spring rolls. We all went to the Battersea branch for Sunday lunch with some friends and their children and three of the children sat very happily on tall chairs looking at the chefs working hard and the chefs were anything but sniffy, engaging the children in repartee and showing them how things worked.

Wok-Wok presents an ideal opportunity for parents to sneak slightly more interesting bits and pieces into their children's diet without them noticing. Even the ice cream had lime, coconut and mango in it, yet they didn't seem to mind. When I passed my notebook to them they were full of enthusiasm. 'Wok-Wok is quite a cool place with groovy music and nice decor,' wrote my young friend Tom. 'The cooks are cool. They talk and make it very fun,' wrote his younger brother.

I suppose, if you're a grandparent, you're looking for a place the children will remember, an event rather than just feeding them up. Sometimes it's better to surrender to kiddyhood and go for the restaurants that lay on crayons and clowns and magic. Smollensky's Balloon has all that and face-painting and Punch and Judy as well. It's so big and noisy you can't tell if your children are misbehaving so they can't embarrass you. And you can drink wine. All this kiddification only goes on at lunchtime on Saturdays and Sundays.

Sticky Fingers, the Bill Wyman place, has good hamburgers. I went there once when it first opened. During Sunday lunch a girl comes round and paints the children's faces. I should have thought the Rolling Stones memorabilia was a bit lost on children, though; like Joe Loss memorabilia. If ever we put a Stones record on the car cassette, ours always complain straight away that it's old music. They can detect it.

I hate McDonalds but the french fries aren't bad and they practically invented chicken nuggets, a great favourite with our children, who also used to quite like being given balloons and worthless gifts when they ordered A Happy Meal, a choice of hamburger, cheeseburger, chicken nuggets or fish fingers plus french fries and a soft drink, for £1.99.

The Rainforest Café near Piccadilly Circus is said to be a great place to take children. A friend of mine went there with her two and particularly liked the high bar-stools shaped like an animal's backside with the appropriate tail hanging down behind. She ordered exotically named cocktails all round. Hers had the gin in it, theirs featured mainly cranberry juice. They ate surrounded by thunder and lightning and tropical rain, with monkeys, elephants, parrots and a particularly alarming gorilla lurking in the dense foliage around their table. Only the parrots are real. She says she enjoyed all that but took against Tracey Tree ('Hi, I'm Tracey Tree . . .') who has a mouth in her trunk and never stopped talking through it; one moment about the destruction of the rainforest and then, in the same caring voice, about the excellent T-shirts and jeans and other jungle-wear they had for sale in their shop.

It was a hot summer's day when we went to Legoland and it has everything a child could possibly want: mazes, railways, boats, rollercoasters, clowns, adventure playgrounds, ferris wheels, horrid things that you sit on and whizz around until you start to feel sick, and a wide range of restaurants, or, as they term them, 'food outlets'.

We chose The Dragon Knight's Castle, north-east of the Wild Woods. It is a proper Robin Hood-style castle, with all the requisite drawbridges, towers, flags, ramparts and so forth and the dining hall is appropriately gloomy. 'Feaste at ye Knight's Table' reads the notice outside. I had the Pork Rolle for £2.45 which consisted of a few slices of squidgy pork in a bread roll. My son had the sweetcorn nuggets which, he said approvingly, tasted like sick to him. Oddly enough they looked quite like it too.

We ate outside, on the castle ramparts, within spitting distance of a troupe of players putting on a show about a break-in at the home of the Three Bears. There was a pleasant free-and-easy air about the place, with no regimentation and none of the usual Disneyland threat of giant Mickey Mouses lumbering into view to intimidate you into smiling. Another smalle plusse pointte: before entering the Knight's Table, I was dreading discovering it was an alcohol-free zone. Happily, this was not the case, and a pleasantly unmedieval Budweiser helped take my mind off what I had just eaten. It was not a Michelin-star experience, but then what Michelin-starred restaurant can offer its guests an in-house Chairoplane?

Certainly attitudes have changed since 1975 when Basil, the co-proprietor of Fawlty Towers, a hotel in Torquay, could be so rude to Ronald, a child dining with his parents in the restaurant.

When Ronald complained that his chips were 'the wrong shape', Basil was bullish in his response. 'Oh dear,' he said, 'what shape do you usually have? Mickey Mouse shape? Smarties shape? Amphibious landing craft shape? *Poke-in-the-eye* shape?'

Now I'd guess that the poke-in-the-eye shape is the only chip still unavailable in some restaurant, somewhere in Britain. One of the few benefits of drink-driving laws is that pubs have to serve food, which means they have to serve families and children. Restaurant chains such as Beefeater (who provide perfectly acceptable food) have become studiously child-friendly, with crayons and things and special children's menus decorated with Mr Men or Teletubbies or even, I daresay, Mickey Mouse. These menus tend to offer dishes of reconstituted chicken or fish all moulded into star-shapes or fish-shapes with gobbledygook kiddy titles. Wimpy, for instance, now offers a choice of a 'benderumptious pork bendy bender meal' or a 'fantabulous fishy nibbles meal'.

The first restaurant I ever visited without a grown-up was a Wimpy. Unlike the restaurants I would visit now and then with my parents, they were unintimidating and they were cheap. Everything came with chips and, perhaps above all else, *you could hold all your food in your hands*. It was my favourite restaurant. I abandoned Wimpy many years ago and when I returned recently with my wife and children I really wanted to find the burgers better than Burger King's burgers, the Jumbolicious Chicken Chunkies far tastier than McDonald's chicken nuggets. But even the children thought the food was disgusting. My daughter said the Jumbolicious Chicken Chunkies tasted as though someone had mixed together loads of salt and a bit of scampi. 'It spreads out in your mouth like a spider's web,' she added.

Sometimes the least likely restaurants are unexpectedly nice to children. I remember going into Michel Roux's Michelin-starred Waterside Inn at Bray with Tallulah when she was a baby and everyone was kind and friendly, producing a high chair and fussing around her as though they were Italians. And Spiga, a sleek and stylish and alarmingly fashionable Soho restaurant which is Italian, but so packed from top to bottom with media types it seemed unlikely they would welcome children, was equally pleasant.

We were lunching with my brother-in-law, who's in advertising, and on his advice I phoned the restaurant manager of Spiga and said diffidently, 'Do you mind children?' Imagine my surprise when he replied instantly, 'We LOVE children!' I almost felt like sending him our children to board there. The children we took along – our two plus two cousins – were indeed greeted as revered customers.

Other nationalities, particularly the British,

tend to think that children and chic occupy two separate planets, each at war with the other. But every Italian restaurant is a family restaurant. The proprietors tend to like children, and so children tend to like them. Growing up in a restaurant culture that accepts them, the children have no need to shriek their defiance from table-tops. At the same time, Italian adults enter restaurants fully expecting the odd child to be running around, never imagining that a few tears from another table will ruin their meal.

I reckon food is not the most important thing about restaurants. I rate the food fourth or fifth. What really matters is the friendliness, particularly with children. When I read the increasingly rare warning, 'No children', in a food guide I speed along to the next entry. Even if I'm not planning to take my own children along, I'm uneasy about entering anywhere so sniffy as to bar them. I prefer the spontaneous to the stuffy, the noisy to the hushed, the joyful to the reverent. And to these ends, I see children as my natural allies.

Addresses

Wok-Wok, 10 Frith Street, London W1 (020 7437 7080) has branches in Fulham, Clapham, Islington, Kensington, Didsbury (Manchester), Nottingham, Marlow and more to follow.

Smollensky's Balloon on the Strand, 105 Strand, London WC2 (020 7497 2101).

Sticky Fingers, 1a Phillimore Gardens, Kensington, London W8 (020 7938 5338).

Rainforest Café, 20 Shaftesbury Avenue, London W1 (020 7434 3111), and 1 The Orient, The Trafford Centre, Manchester M17 (0161 747 1122).

Legoland, Windsor Park, Winkfield Road, Windsor, Berkshire (0870 504 0404).

The Waterside Inn, Ferry Road, Bray, Berkshire (0162 862 0691).

Spiga, 84–86 Wardour Street, London W1 (020 7734 3444).

McDonalds, Beefeater and Wimpy have branches throughout the country.

Joan Bakewell Speaks

Joan Bakewell, well known as a television arts presenter, is now the Chair of The British Film Institute. She is sixty-six and lives in London with her second husband, the film-producer Jack Emery. They have two groups of five grandchildren, aged between eight and three.

My father was dying of cancer when Thomas, my oldest grandchild, was born. Matthew and Sally, my son and daughter-in-law, dashed to his bedside with the baby as soon as they could and we all stood around the bed realising that, briefly, we were four generations together. My father had been determined to stay alive to see the baby and he died two days later. At the same time Thomas's birth made me a grandmother and my father's death moved me on a generation.

Three of my grandchildren live in Dorset and two live in Bristol. I want to stay as close as possible to all of them for at least the first ten years which I believe to be a time of huge change in children's lives, so I try and visit them every few weeks and they come and stay with Jack and me in London.

I'm far stricter than their parents. My grandchildren are all aware that grandma is old, that her house is ordered and that she doesn't like a lot of noise. But they also know that I organise terrific outings to the zoo or the theatre. We always holiday together, renting a cottage in the same Cornish village where I used to take my children, so it is full of memories for us all – very nostalgic.

Jack and I have busy careers but we always try to keep space in our diaries during school holidays and half-terms. It does mean forgoing some income but I think family ties are far more important.

" ONE FOR MOMMY, ONE FOR DADDY,
ONE FOR MUMMY'S PARTNER
ONE FOR DADDY'S PARTNER
ONE FOR HER LITTLE BOY
ONE FOR YOUR STEP-SISTER ....."

11

Relationships

Well, all I can say about the Hopi Indians is that they had a nice sense of irony. Or maybe their grandmothers really were sweet-natured and wise enough for the tribal heads to nod in agreement and declare truthfully: 'When the grandmothers speak the earth will be healed.'

Not most of the grandmothers I know. When my mother's mother spoke it was anything but a healing experience. A telephone call from granny set sister against sister, renewing old sibling rivalries and kindling internecine feuds which simmered resentfully for years; from what I hear, ours was not a unique family experience.

Novelist Julie Myerson once wrote in the *Independent* that after the break-up of her parents' marriage her father and paternal grandmother had no further contact with her or her sisters. 'The last time I saw granny, I cycled four miles to take her a bunch of buttercups picked in the hedgerows. "Thanks for the weeds," she said.' Julie was then six years old. She was almost grown-up when her grandmother died. 'We later heard she'd had photos of us by her bed. Pictures of three little girls frozen in time.'

Of course there are grandmothers, like you and me and all those quoted in these pages, who are capable of loving diplomacy – keeping our mouths shut when it matters. And I know two sets of mothers and daughters-in-law who have taken Naomi and Ruth's 'whithersoever thou goest I will go' biblical pledge to selfless lengths. In one case the grandmother sold her house and moved from Surrey up to Yorkshire (where her widowed daughter-in-law was a teacher) so that she was on hand to look after her grandchildren. In the other case the step-daughter is preparing to sacrifice her farmhouse kitchen (plus Aga and pantry and cloakrooms and gun-room) to turn it into a garden flat for her mother-in-law who is becoming increasingly frail in mind and limb.

And there's a lovely lady called Fleurice I met in Florida who showed me a photograph of her son, often away on duty in the US Navy, and his beautiful wife. 'He married this sweet girl I'd hardly met who phoned me up a year later and said: "Come quickly, I'm having the baby and there's no one to help." ' Fleurice, a senior executive in the health department, delegated instantly. 'I flew right across the States,' she said, 'and eighteen hours later I was panting companionably with this girl I hardly knew.'

My own mother would drop everything to stand in when my childcare arrangements fell apart and, although she loathed the sound of bagpipes and swore they brought on her migraine, she once spent a whole afternoon loyally playing and replaying Jimmy Shand records when my step-daughters were going through their Scottish dancing phase.

Unfortunately, not all grandmothers are so kind and accommodating. Some grandmothers relish a family feud and, like any other member of the female sex, know instinctively where to insert the knife to cause maximum irritation or distress. There's many a grand-mother who has let fall a casual remark or apparently caring piece of advice over the tea-table, and then gone home leaving the grandchildren in tears and their mothers and fathers at each other's throats.

These little snatches of dialogue may sound inoffen-sive enough, but can you decipher the troublemaking subtext of what granny is really saying?

When she says: 'Oh, you look exhausted, my dear. Can I give you a help with your ironing?' she is really saying to her career daughter-in-law who brings home upwards of £50,000 a year: 'Just because you go out enjoying yourself at all those business lunches doesn't mean you can neglect to iron my son's shirts.'

When she says: 'No wonder you've caught another cold, darling, when you won't wear a vest', she is really saying to her son, a company director and father of three: 'Mother knows what's best for her little boy.'

When she says: 'Ah, I see you've moved the television over there. Jean always used to have it on the shelf by the fire', she is really saying to her son's new second wife: 'You've only been married to him for a month and already you're changing everything dear Jean arranged so beautifully.'

When she says: 'Isn't that Julia Roberts, the one who was in that film with Richard Thingy . . . you remember . . . doesn't she remind you of someone? I know, that girl who used to work in the shop next to the cleaners when we lived in Hastings . . . it's the hair . . .' she is really saying to her grandchildren, who have been allowed to stay up specially to watch *Notting Hill* on the telly: 'Why do you want to bother with that silly old film when granny is here?'

When she says: 'I thought I'd take Claudia over to Paris on Eurostar next week – she deserves a little treat', she is really saying to her son-in-law: 'You've got time to play golf every weekend at that expensive club of yours, but you never seem to have the time or money to take my daughter anywhere.'

When she says: 'Oh, you should just see our Jennifer's Tom. Such a lovely baby. Sleeps right through the night. She breastfeeds him, of course', she is really saying to another of her daughters: 'Your sister, Jennifer, is a better mother than you are.'

When she says: 'Why don't you all come over on Sunday and I'll cook a proper roast with all the trimmings', she is really saying to her son's partner, a vegetarian: 'Nobody ever gets a decent meal in this house.'

When she says: 'Where *do* you find all those clever presents? Johnny's had so much fun with the electric car. We took it to the park twice last week and all the other children wanted a go on it', she is really saying to The Other Granny: 'You may buy our grandson expensive presents but, unlike me, you are only a visiting granny.'

Even husbands and fathers, who might well be the only family members not to pick up on this feminine double-talk, will have realised that mothers and daughters-in-law often have a tricky relationship, particularly where the grandchildren are concerned. A recent study at Cambridge University found that although today's mothers-in-law approved the equality of women in general, in practice they felt that the wellbeing of their sons and grandchildren should come before the wife's career. The most common complaint from the daughters-in-law was that doting mothers who have spent a lifetime spoiling their sons expected the wife to do the same. 'If a man asks for the butter, his mother goes and gets it,' said the social psychologist who carried out the research.

Jackie Stallone is such a mother. When her son, Sylvester, announced that he was going to marry his pregnant lover, Jennifer Flavin, Mrs Stallone said: 'In my eyes, no woman is good enough for Sylvester.' She then added, unkindly and unwisely: 'He shouldn't walk down the aisle with that girl. Jennifer is in love all right, but with the idea of being important. I think there's a mean streak in her.'

I don't know whether the baby turned out to be a boy or a girl, but either way this is one granny whose daughter-in-law won't be eager to invite her round to admire the grandchild.

A friend phoned the other day to point out what a mistake she'd made having sons instead of daughters. 'What I hadn't realised', she said, 'is that you are not only a grandmother, you are a mother-in-law and it's only natural that when a young girl has a baby she turns to her mother. I've never been jealous of anything or anyone in my life, and suddenly there's this other woman standing in the middle of the kitchen, plump and grey-haired, a proper grandma. I know my grandson adores her, it's always "Grandma this" and "Grandma that" and I'm Sue, which I insisted on being called and wish I hadn't. And I hate her, poor woman.

'And now my family is going to live near that wretched grandmother and she's got a big old house in the middle of fields and there are horses and dogs. I can't speak . . . I can't speak about it.' My friend said she was aiming to be sparkling and glamorous and hoped that the grandchildren would turn out very cerebral and loathe the country and want to come and do urban things with her in London.

Grandmotherly emotions run deep, and a telephone call saying, 'Don't bother to come over on Thursday, mum, Tim's mother has kindly offered to take the children to Alton Towers', will have the cancelled granny plotting, at the very least, a competitive trip to Disneyland.

Goodness knows, traditional relationships are hard enough without the complication of half of all marriages ending in divorce, adding and subtracting family members and intensifying the anxieties of both adults and children. As Mark Steyn, writing in the *Spectator* about divorce, American-style, put it: 'A generation of American children has learned to keep its suitcase packed and a bundle of change-of-address cards on hand.'

You don't think, do you, when you meet this wonderful man and you fall in love and your children get on brilliantly with his children, and his ex-wife marries a man with three more children, and then they have two of their own, and your ex-husband takes up with an earth-mother of five, that thirty years on you'll be trying to fit this extended family into your living room?

And when you've finally managed to remember the name of your husband's ex-wife's second daughter, worked out the social etiquette of who to invite to family parties and who should, on no account, be invited with them, and found it just about possible to speak to your ex-husband's wife without curling your lip, your children and step-children start getting divorced, too.

Your son, looking shifty, says surely you must have realised that he and Kate (the daughter-in-law you supported through labour pains and with whom you shared your first box of Persil Washing Tablets) have not been getting on too well for some time now and no, of course there isn't anyone else.

Kate goes to live near her mother, taking your eight-year-old granddaughter with her, and in her place appears Joanne, who looks just like Kate only younger, with a fresh set of children who are plunged into this mêlée of new relatives without any knowledge of family history or house rules, poor little things. 'In this house, Jason, we take off our outdoor shoes when we come in from the garden, and we never turn on the television before six o'clock.'

Victoria Wood had a hilarious sketch about a stranger catapulted into somebody else's Christmas: 'Oh, we always go up to the top of the hill behind the house on Christmas Eve and sing *The Sound of Music*'; and just imagine the horror of turning up at Sandringham for Christmas with something lavishly gift-wrapped from Asprey, only to discover that the Royal Christmas tradition is to compete to see who has spent the least. Evidently Princess Anne won the contest one year by giving Prince Charles a doormat.

Mary and Dick Francis's older son, Merrick, has

been married three times. 'I've had three daughters-in-law and I've liked them all and regretted the break-ups,' Mary says. 'I wouldn't take sides, it's awfully bad for the children. Relationships with exes are difficult and all one can do with the grandchildren is not discuss it. Dick and I have been married for fifty years; it's just a matter of luck. We acquired step-grandchildren with the last wife. Of course it's quite different to meet a child at nine instead of knowing her from birth and I think the eldest child did feel quite alienated in our family to start with. Now she's in her twenties and she's become integrated and grown into an enormously warm, friendly person.'

Art dealer Angela Flowers has five children, nine grandchildren (including her eldest son's third wife's daughter who said, 'Please can I call you granny?'), one son-in-law, three current daughters-in-law, and five ex-daughters-in-law. 'Sixteen years ago my third son's partner conceived just before they separated and he didn't want to see the baby, a daughter,' she says. 'I felt I had to stay in touch with her and her mother and because of that I got blamed for all the tensions and anything that went wrong in the following two rela-tionships. But it was worth it. He's seeing his daughter now and he's delighted with her, so that's good.

'I absolutely adore babies and my sons always ring up and say, "You'd better hurry, mum, if you're going to do the first nappy." One of my grandsons was born in Australia and I went out there a fortnight after the birth. I was not welcome. That particular daughter-in-law was very bitchy. I was holding the baby and she came in, shouting, "What have you done to him?" Now she's married again and is therefore happier and more relaxed and we're all going to see the grandson at Christmas.

'I do have to be a bit careful what I say. Even a little bit careful of saying, "How's mum?" to the grandchild when the current step-mum is present.'

A friend who has four grandchildren of her own and seven step-grandchildren says she finds keeping up with birthday and Christmas presents a full-time career. 'My own grandchildren get on very well with my step-grandchildren and there's no problem. Unless', she adds with significant emphasis, 'their other grandmother is with them. I treat the step-grandchildren like mine, although you can't help making comparisons. Usually adverse ones. I find myself thinking, "Oh, Jonathan isn't nearly as bright as our little Oliver." '

There are harrowing tales of grandparents who have lost their grandchildren through divorce and travel miles to catch a glimpse of them coming out of school; or grandparents who have gone to court to ask for visitation rights and are only allowed four meetings a year in a grim hall under the watchful eye of a social worker, instead of being able to take them out to McDonalds or let them run about in the sunshine. 'What about children's rights?' one of these alienated grandmothers asked on *Woman's Hour*. She said that she loved her grandchildren far too much to go to court, so she writes them a letter once a month, full of family news, and files it away. One day, when the grandchildren are grown up, she'll give them the letters.

When marriages collapse it is often the grandparents who keep families together and give children stability and reassurance. One granny had her own grandchildren and their new step-siblings to tea together and bent over backwards to treat them equally. The step-grandchildren behaved like little angels and her own two created mayhem. It was revealed, much later, that at a time when they were most insecure about their relationship with their mother and father, they felt they were no longer special to their own granny, either.

Another granny invited her grandchildren on their own and received a stinging telephone call from the new wife: 'I'm expected to be a full-on 24-hours-a-day mother to your grandchildren and you can't even bother to have my children for one afternoon.'

It is not always easy being a grandmother and it's an even more difficult role to play if the grandchildren are not your blood relatives. All the more heart-warming, then, when an eight-year-old new step-granddaughter puts her hand in yours and says, 'I'm very lucky. I've got three nans now.'

Leslie Kenton Speaks

Leslie Kenton, health guru, novelist and photographer is fifty-eight, the daughter of jazz man Stan Kenton and the mother of four children all by different fathers. She has one grandchild, Attica, who is one.

I was pregnant with Branton, my eldest, when I was seventeen, so I could have been a grandmother when I was thirty-five; but none of my children got married and then, when they did, they didn't have children. It was therefore a surprise when Attica was born.

The children said, 'What do you want to be called?' and I said, 'I don't care, but not gran or nan, thank you.' I'm the last person in the world to think of myself as a grandmother. I never felt my own children belonged to me, but were unique individuals I was lucky enough to be looking after. I'm very passionate about the people I care for, but very detached as well.

I think I will be an adviser of some kind to Attica. Someone who will keep him in line. I've never indulged children, I can't take badly behaved children. And if they are in my house I don't have a problem, they just do as I say.

For instance, I had a friend staying with his child and at lunch the child looked at her melon and said, in a weedy, whiny voice, 'I don't like melon.' 'Yes you do,' her father said. 'You know you do. You loved melon when we had it at uncle's house.'

The child screamed, left the room and ran upstairs and slammed the door. I followed her and said, 'We do not scream or slam doors in this house.'

Oh, you wouldn't believe it. I'm real nasty, real heavy when it comes to discipline.

" RUN UPSTAIRS AND GET MY SPECTACLES, DEAR ....
YOUR HEELS ARE LOWER THAN MINE."

12

Grantastic!

A grantastic grandmother has broad horizons and an
open mind and is more inclined to drive across The
Empty Quarter for her holidays than book up again at
'that nice quiet hotel in Bournemouth'.

A grantastic grandmother

- is a reliable backstop but is not always there, waiting
  at the end of the phone, like a new lover, for the
  grandchildren to ring and say they're coming over;
- shops for the latest MP3 player by searching the

internet, gets her shoes from Manolo Blahnik and
goes to Space N.K. instead of Superdrug for her
shampoo;

- never, ever says: 'Have you got a kiss for granny?'
- learns First Aid so that she is calm and in control if
  a grandson gets a bone stuck in his throat or a
  granddaughter breaks a collarbone;
- lies: 'I'm fine thanks', when the grandchildren ask
  her how she is, instead of giving them the details
  of her arthritis, joint by joint;
- never, ever says: 'Pop upstairs and get my glasses,
  dear. Your legs are younger than mine';
- trades in her Vauxhall for a SMART and gets
  copped for speeding in it;
- books a table at the newest 'in' restaurant and
  invites the grandchildren without their parents;
- never, ever says: 'I expect I seem very old to you';
- knows the names of the grandchildren's hamsters
  and doesn't go 'eugh' or scream when she's allowed
  to hold a white rat or a lizard;
- initiates games which involve her crawling through
  the undergrowth or plunging through the surf;
- takes the grandchildren to see Father Christmas in
  Lapland instead of Selfridges;
- never, ever says: 'I think it's going to rain today, I
  can feel it in my bones';
- is thinner than The Other Granny.

This woman is absolutely nothing like the familiar
image of a grandmother popularised in magazines and

television soaps and newspapers. 'OAP mugged in shopping precinct' I read in my paper, and I'm just visualising this poor old soul with blood seeping through her tight, grey curls, when I realise that she's younger than me. And then there's all that subversive, whimsical stuff written in heart-warming mini-booklets and inside cards that have 'To a Grandmother' printed on the front.

How about this, for instance?

Always treat your granny like a greenhouse plant, kept warm in the sun and with plenty to drink. Give her lots of photographs for her albums and photo frames. Invite her to stay and furnish her with bed-socks, a nightcap and hot water bottle and in the morning a cup of tea or breakfast in bed with flowers on the tray . . . help her by running errands and finding her spectacles and knitting. Always compliment your granny on her cooking . . .*

Well, the only bit of that I'd go along with is the nightcap and I bet they mean Horlicks rather than double malt. Hard to believe, but somebody has actually printed this patronising rubbish onto the back of a decorative tea towel and I only hope that any child giving this to her grandmother will be cut swiftly out of her will and made to do the washing up. There's

*Sheila Kitzinger deplored this 'saccharine folk wisdom' in her book, *Becoming a Grandmother* (Pocket Books, £7.99).

more of it in the same vein, and every word conveys the message that a grandmother is frail, foolish and past it.

Not an enticing role model, is it? And yet there are far too many women who, when they first draw their pension or become a widow or a grandmother, feel so diminished that they believe this is how they are destined to be from now on. They may not wear bedsocks but they are probably gazing pensively at the modern equivalent, which are Marks and Spencer's comfy footgloves. Wear those for a week and you'll be unable ever again to slip your feet into slim, elegant footwear.

As the balance of power tilts inevitably towards the next generation, these women allow themselves to be shunted out of the mainstream of life into a quiet backwater where the peak experience is watching Michael Barrymore on television once a week. In no time at all they become non-persons, the people you don't notice in the supermarket or the street, as anonymous as those elderly peasants, camouflaged in identical black, who toil in the Mediterranean sun and turn out, when you get to know them, to be forty-two.

There were a great many women like that in the last two generations, and not so many now, thank goodness, who were brought up in an era when you were expected to scrimp and save and sacrifice yourself for your children and your grandchildren and it was considered sinful to spend anything on yourself. 'Don't you worry about me' was their mantra.

If you offered to paint their dingy front room or buy them a new outfit or a hat to replace the rigidly plaited grey chiffon model, circa 1945, or take them away for a fortnight in the Caribbean sunshine, they would draw closer to the two-bar electric fire and say gloomy things like, 'Oh no, dear, it will see me out . . .' – 'I've got more clothes than I'll ever need . . .' – 'Not at my age, dear.'

They didn't realise how depressing they were, how their children dreaded the duty visits, phoning each other up every August to confirm 'It's your turn to have mother next Christmas, don't forget', and how guilty this made the children feel. The irony is that these were mothers who would cut their throats for their family but were incapable of being joyful for them.

Luckily, most of us these days have a healthy streak of selfishness which stops us embracing this kind of self-inflicted ageism, but it does still exist. Katharine Whitehorn, who writes a trenchant Agony Aunt column in *Saga* magazine, says: 'The difference between people who strike one as past it and the ones who, though they may be older, are still good value, is often a question of how much they have, or have not, limited themselves. People can get depressingly set in their ways. They don't go out on Bank Holidays because of the traffic, or in the rush hour; nine in the morning is too early and four too late in winter; Tuesday is their day for changing their library books. Before you know it, they can only do anything on alternate Thursdays, if it isn't raining. One longs for some outside force to come in and shake them up a bit.'

She gets tearful letters from women who feel that they have been excluded from the special family days when they want to be with their grandchildren; perhaps a daughter-in-law and her jolly, boisterous family have hijacked Christmas, leaving the other granny alone and ignored. Katharine's advice is to be proactive. 'Institute some occasions of your own which also have their place in the calendar and have to be respected – regular granny days when you take the children to an ice show or on a yearly picnic. If you've got the money, use it to buy treats. We all know how boring a cruise can be on your own but if you take the grandchildren along they'll enjoy the dancing, the sight-seeing trips and the swimming pool and you'll have fun, too.'

Really, there's no reason for most of us to mope about, suspecting slights and humbly expecting to be sidelined. Of course there are elderly people trying to make do on their state pensions, but for those with mortgage-free houses and private pensions and free or subsidised fares and the NHS or private health insurance to fall back on, things have never been so good. We're living longer, staying healthier and although you may not have realised it, with all those thigh-high skirts and tank tops in the stores, the fifty-to-sixty-four-year-old age group now spend more than anyone else on fashion.

Are we spending wisely? Not, I think, if we slavishly

follow the latest craze. I am not, obviously, thinking bare midriffs or the new 'hot pants' here, but even the popular pashmina was a doubtful idea. A waif-like Kate Moss lookalike draped in a pashmina might be OK, although I'm not totally sure about this, but you and I similarly draped would have all the allure of Whistler's Mother.

It may be appallingly superficial, but we are judged on our appearance – and why not, since everyone else is? With this in mind, consider these basic ground rules.

Any garment (or shoe) prefaced by the word 'classic' means it's outdated and dreary, particularly if it is followed by the words, 'two-piece' or 'three-piece'.

Baggy shirts and tunics worn over trousers do not conceal a multitude of sins unless they are unusually well cut; otherwise they lodge on a large bottom as though on a convenient shelf, revealing from the back precise measurements of hip and thigh.

The no-make-up look actually means putting on more make-up but with subtlety, using all the concealers and wrinkle-reducers and extra-firming creams and luminous foundations you can afford. Heavy face-powder clogs unkindly in what we like to think of as laughter lines, and lipsticks in vivid shades of pensioner purple are a killer on anyone, particularly a pensioner.

Just because some man said in 1962, 'You should always wear your hair like that, it suits you' doesn't mean you should still be going around in a time warp looking like Jean Shrimpton's grandmother. Get a good haircut and shun heated rollers or anything that encourages a bouffant.

Plastic surgery? Why not, if you're simply raising a drooping eyelid or erasing an under-eye wrinkle? But before considering the full facelift or tummy tuck, do think of the depressing way even the toughest leather tends to sag and wrinkle when it's stretched.

The best fashion tip of all, at any age? Lose half a stone or whatever it takes to get into a regular size twelve or fourteen; then you can do what every other well-dressed woman does, which is to wear what you look and feel good in. It all depends on your lifestyle and where you live. A friend who lives in London and the country says that when she had blonde streaks put in her hair, her country friends said, with a note of disapproval in their voices: 'Oh, you've dyed your hair.' And when the streaks grew out, the London friends said: 'Oh, you've stopped dyeing your hair', in a tone she understood to mean, 'Oh, you've let yourself go.'

Grandchildren are equally frank. 'Why have you got hairs in your nose?' and 'Why do you smell funny?' and 'Why does your bosom hang down?' One is tempted to snap back: 'Why are you such a rude little girl?' (it's usually the granddaughter rather than the grandson who has the sharp eye and tongue), but, of course, the child's questions are spot on.

Katharine Whitehorn says she despairs of the women who don't bother to pluck long white hairs from their chins and the men with greasy hair or grubby clothes. 'The world does not warm, either, to older people who have permanently disgruntled expressions,' she says. 'No doubt in everybody's lives there are things which really make them miserable, but it's pointless to spend time getting indignant about things we cannot possibly affect. Maybe the young do have no manners these days, the politicians even less sense and the weather forecasts less reliability than ever, but it isn't worth disapproving of them if our disgust changes nothing but our own expressions.'

I wasn't surprised to read the other day yet another piece of medical research discovering the obvious: that cheery optimists live longer than gloomy pessimists. Certainly all the contented older women I know don't pretend to be younger than they are but have a youthful, positive attitude to whatever the world hurls at them. If they are widowed or divorced they don't sit around helplessly, hoping that another man will seek them out and cherish them and fill in their tax forms; they get involved in something new.

A fifty-four-year-old divorced neighbour of mine sprang onto the Paris catwalk to model one of Vivienne Westwood's collections; a seventy-year-old friend learned to paint after her husband died and three years later had her own show, and a friend, long since divorced, who had always been a good cook, found herself at a loose end and started applying for all those 'Housekeeper wanted' ads in the back of *The Lady*. Last time I heard from her she was running a large house in Gloucestershire and was just about to quit that job for another in Ibiza. Others have taken up voluntary work, or travelled to the places they'd always longed to visit and never had the time or money to do before. And one grandmother surprised us all and delighted her daughter-in-law, a busy doctor, by becoming a full-time nanny to her granddaughter.

These women are all too busy getting on with their lives to fall into the old person's traditional trap of translating money into a worry, like brooding about how to leave their savings to the grandchildren so that their son's second wife's family don't get hold of it. They call in professional advice and then study the financial pages and make up their own minds.

I notice there's a new scheme around which links children's savings with baby-food products. You collect tokens of £5 and £10 along with the food and these are credited to the child's account. This scheme is obviously aimed at fond grandparents, but you don't have to be a merchant banker to work out that either you or the baby will have to eat a lot of rusks and puréed vegetables to get a halfway decent deal. Women who say they don't understand money, and I am one of them, are like women who can't change plugs. 'Don't want to' is what we really mean.

Money, Katharine Whitehorn tells her readers, is there to be enjoyed, not worried about. 'I know a grandmother living frugally on maintenance,' she says, 'who inherited £2,000 and splashed out on a fur-lined mackintosh and a marvellous black suede trouser suit that lifted her wardrobe and her spirits for years.'

Really, there is only one word to describe this imprudent, frivolously extravagant, joyfully optimistic grandmother. The word is Grantastic!

Barbara Follett Speaks

Barbara Follett, fifty-seven, is the Labour Member of Parliament for Stevenage and is married to the novelist Ken Follett. She has three children, two step-children and two grandchildren – Alexandra who is six and Clementine, twenty months.

When my grandchildren were born I was pleased and then surprised by the realisation of how much time had passed. It seems like only yesterday that I had my children. Now they were having their own.

I see the grandchildren at least once or twice a week and we spend part of the Christmas, Easter and summer holidays together. About twice a month they come and spend the weekend with us in Stevenage, my constituency. They have their own bedroom with bunk beds decorated to look like a red double-decker London bus. They also have a tree house and swings in the garden. It gives me great pleasure to do things for them which I was never able to afford to do for my own children.

Usually, we go for long walks in Knebworth Park with Custard and Bess, our two labradors, and Perdie, their poodle. We play games like Snap and Memory, watch *101 Dalmatians* again and again and read books of all kinds. Alexandra loves Harry Potter and Clementine is seriously into the Mr Men series. I sing songs (badly) with them while their grandfather Ken plays along on the guitar.

I think a grandparent's role is to support and back up the parents as well as being a pleasure-giver and occasional spoiler. I go shopping with Alexandra and Clementine, ostensibly to buy presents for their parents but actually to buy presents for them. I let them rummage about in my cupboards to find clothes, shawls and scarves for dressing-up games, and allow Alexandra to go through my jewel box. And I do try not to answer yes to every 'Can I have this when you are dead, Baba?' question.

I also talk to them a lot about the family. It's very important to me and, I hope, to them. My husband Ken is their step-grandfather and he is writing a history of the family for them. Their own grandfather was assassinated in South Africa twenty-two years ago. Alexandra knows about this and sometimes asks me what Grandad Richard was like. I am happy to tell her he was a brave man. It is very difficult for her to understand why people wanted him dead.

Death has been very present recently. Ken's mother died last year and my own mother, Granny Lee, died early this year. Alexandra and Clementine came to the funeral in South Africa. They played contentedly in the rock pools on the beach as we committed my mother's ashes to the sea. The weather was chilly and Clementine was carried back to the car wrapped in my mother's shawl, the same one that had covered the box holding her ashes a few minutes earlier. It gave me a great sense of the continuity of life.

"...CAN I HAVE THIS WHEN YOU'RE DEAD?"